LIVED THROUGH THIS

Lived Through This

Listening to the Stories
of Sexual Violence Survivors

Anne K. Ream
with photographs by Patricia Evans

BEACON PRESS, BOSTON

Beacon Press
Boston, Massachusetts
www.beacon.org

Beacon Press books
are published under the auspices of
the Unitarian Universalist Association of Congregations.

18 17 16 15   8 7 6 5 4 3 2

This book is printed on acid-free paper that meets the uncoated paper ANSI/NISO
specifications for permanence as revised in 1992.

Text design by Ruth Maassen

Library of Congress Cataloging-in-Publication Data
Ream, Anne K.
  Lived through this : listening to the stories of sexual-violence survivors / Anne K.
Ream ; with photographs by Patricia Evans.
     pages cm
  ISBN 978-0-8070-3930-4 (paperback) ISBN 978-0-8070-3336-4 (hardcover) ISBN
978-0-8070-3337-1 (ebook) 1. Sexual abuse victims—Case studies. 2. Sex crimes—
Case studies. I. Title.
  HV6556.R43 2014
  362.8830973—dc23
                              2013045411

For Clifton

"Behind the story I tell is the one I don't. Behind the story you hear is the one I wish I could make you hear."

—DOROTHY ALLISON,
Two or Three Things I Know for Sure

"What if memories were just memories, without any consolatory or persecutory power? Would they exist at all, or was it always emotional pressure that summoned images from what was potentially all of experience so far?"

—EDWARD ST. AUBYN, *At Last*

CONTENTS

New Rules for Radicals

It's (Not) All About the Children

INTRODUCTION

"Hope," Flannery O'Connor wrote, in her recently published diaries, "can only be realized through despair." Our emotional lives are characterized by feelings that appear to be contradictory but are often co-dependent. We most long for freedom after we've been fearful, peace after a period of restlessness, words when we've been told, for too long, to be silent. Our desires—our hopes—are our histories unmasked.

This book is a story of hope. In its pages, you'll meet a community of rape and sexual violence survivors—gorgeous, accomplished, funny, all-too-human women and men—who have been shaped, but refuse to be defined, by their histories of violence. They are brave, and they are outspoken—these qualities are perhaps self-evident—but mostly they are hopeful. The hope at the heart of these stories has less to do with the narratives themselves, however moving and even inspirational they may be, and more to do with the fact that these survivors are here to tell them.

The sharing of a story, especially a story of having survived rape or sexual abuse, is inherently an act of faith in the listener. We do not testify to our experiences because it is healing—although it can be—but because it is necessary in a world that too often underestimates the scope and scale of sexual violence. The women and men in these pages are believers in the power of testimony—and in the power of you.

This book is a story of hope, and of truth. There is nothing beautiful about the violence that has been visited on the survivors profiled in these pages. Violence in the real world far, far away from a Quentin Tarantino film, is never beautiful. Returning imaginatively to the place where someone has been harmed is painful—and it should be. But through the lives that they are living today, the survivors in this book remind us of all that remains possible in the wake of the terrible.

Separately, each of these stories can be read as an account of an individual who lived through sexual violence and emerged changed but intact. Collectively, they are something greater: a window into a world where rape and abuse are breathtakingly commonplace. Sexual violence is the ultimate shape-shifter. Today it is rape in the United States military, tomorrow female genital cutting, next the trafficking of women and girls around the corner and across the globe. Yet all violence is characterized by one constant: it will leave devastation and loneliness in its wake.

Loneliness is the quality I most associate with my own history of violence. For all of the ugly details of the night when I was kidnapped and raped, the memory that remains most powerful for me is not of the violence itself, or the exhausting and stupid degradations—*you bitch, you whore, if you say a word, I'm going to kill you*—but of the distant sound of a neighbor's stereo playing Madonna's "Lucky Star" as I was assaulted. Years later, I found a way to distance myself from that moment, turning it into irony—"Madonna! I was a Clash and Bowie girl, so it was such an indignity"—but in reality, that Madonna song, however banal, became the outside world to me. Her music was a stand-in for life itself, a reminder of all of the frivolous things I wished for and suddenly stood to lose. I knew as I listened to that song that I was no longer of the world, but outside it, watching myself being raped, knowing that if I lived, I could never go back to the place I was before.

Hearing the sounds outside of my apartment that night—the voices floating in from the street, the playing of a pop song I loathed but suddenly wanted to hear a thousand times more—was unbearably sad. I have never felt, before or since, more alone. When I was released hours later, the sheer joy I felt rivaled nothing I had ever known. It was the joy of life being returned to me, the sense that however altered I might be, I was still there. In the months and years that followed, I sometimes longed for that moment of first freedom. I was at a turning point but could not yet see the difficult points in the road ahead. I knew that I was going to live, yet had only an inkling of how different my life would be. It was a perfect, temporary elation.

I come from a family that believes in the power of silences. "You don't have to tell all that you know," my grandmother would tell us. Her words were meant to encourage humility, but they carried with them the faintest whiff of a warning: the world would be kinder to me, and I more appealing to it, if I kept to a minimum the exposure of any uncomfortable truths. Like her monogrammed black cashmere sweaters, her ever-present pink lipstick, or her good jewelry, this was silence as a form of presentation: a way of showing the world who you were by declining to speak of what you had lived through. Such an imperative took on a new and troubling significance after I lived through rape.

People are comfortable with—even encourage—the silence and invisibility of those who have survived sexual violence. When the mainstream media covers rape, it most often declines to use the names or show the faces of victims, a necessary practice that protects privacy, even as it renders us faceless and further isolated. Of course, privacy is a small and important mercy to offer to those who have already lost so much, and rape victims choose anonymity for a variety of psychological, practical, and professional reasons. But anonymity does not lend itself to community, and it was a community of survivors, with a community's collective power to challenge a world in which such violence exists, that photographer Patricia Evans—herself a survivor of rape—and I went in search of when we began the project that became *Lived Through This.*

According to a comprehensive World Health Organization report released in 2013, one in three women across the globe has been a victim of rape or physical abuse. One in five women in the United States will be raped at some point in their lifetime. Nearly one in six boys will live through rape or sexual abuse before they turn eighteen. Yet when we encounter these crimes, we experience a sort of blindness. The violence that is before us should not be difficult to discern—its symptoms and signs are often quite visible—but because it is easier for our psyche and conscience, we choose, and it is often a choice, not to see. Thus the devastation that is childhood sexual abuse becomes a "family affair," the near-epidemic rates of rape at colleges and universities merely part of "campus life," and rape and torture during armed conflict part of the inevitable, expected "messiness of war." Behind these euphemisms are the stories you are about to read, stories that make the human costs of violence painfully clear.

I have spent most of my adult life in the presence of a shadow self. I am a woman who has lived through rape, haunted by the specter of the person I might have been if I had never known such violence. I am deeply in love with my life—perhaps more in love than I might have been had I not come so close to losing it—and I have had the rare privilege of living that life fully and with more joy than I once thought possible.

None of this has stopped me from wondering who I might have been if I had never been raped. Wanting my pre-rape self back has been a senseless, impossible exercise, but the longing, like most unrequited longing, has been difficult to shake. Yet in the writing of this book, as I have listened to and learned from the remarkable women and men you are about to encounter—and many others not in these pages—my two selves have finally come together. How can I wish for the person I was when it is the person I am who has been entrusted with the telling of these stories?

Keep Calm and Carry On

It didn't take long for the advice to flow the way wine flows at a dinner party that begins at eight and continues into the wee hours: slowly and carefully at first, and then in an insistent torrent.

I'd never before realized how often—and with what enthusiasm—well-intentioned people bandy about the phrase "you should." Who doesn't hate the directive, really? It's so smug, so certain, so relentless in its implication that there is a magic bullet for whatever ails you if only you'll do as someone else suggests. In the wake of any sort of public trauma or grief, you'll encounter plenty of unknowns, and at least one certainty: the advice givers will come out in force. *You should talk about it. You should forget about it. You need therapy. You need God. You should blame God. Are you taking enough bubble baths?*

I was twenty-five years old when I was kidnapped and raped. I had the good fortune, if it can be called that, of being attacked near the end of November. This meant that once I had dealt with the preliminaries required of a victim who has decided to press charges against her assailant—vacating the home that had become a crime scene, submitting to police and FBI interviews, viewing a lineup of suspects, meeting with the US attorney assigned to my case—I could return to our family home in the suburbs of Chicago, taking time off during a month when I would not be missed at my recently secured dream job working for a Washington, DC, lobbying and communications firm. Back in Wheaton, Illinois, surrounded by friends and family who were aware of "what I had gone through"—a euphemism for rape that people seemed to find comforting—I was deluged with opinions on what *should* happen next. And, far more troublingly, what was *going* to happen next.

What was going to happen, it became clear as I listened to the well-intentioned around me, wasn't good. I had suffered a "traumatic experience," and I would now need "a lot of professional help": a support group, a rape crisis center, and a regimen of talk therapy, for starters. There was much discussion about how it might be a good idea for me to quit my job and come back to the Midwest, since my work was "so stressful," even without "all that you have to deal with now," and of course, it was presumed, "you won't want to return to *that city*" (suddenly Washington, DC, like the rape itself, could be referred to only euphemistically). An alternative to coming back to Chicago was suggested, rather hopefully. Perhaps I might move to New Haven, where my longtime boyfriend was in graduate school. Surely marriage was on the horizon, and wouldn't a campus far away from Washington be a good place to heal?

There seemed to be consensus, and it was this: what had happened to me was awful—awful in a way that was not ordinary. So I was going to be screwed up for a long, long time. And if I didn't make recovery the focus of my life during the months ahead, I was going to be screwed up even longer.

The truth is that at that time I more or less believed this grim prognosis. During the first weeks after my assault, I was shocked and overwhelmed, tired all the time but never able to rest. I acclimated to a new sort of fear, the fear that one feels after a violence you've only seen in films has made its way into your life. The unthinkable had happened, which meant the unthinkable might happen again. At night, I would dream about the attack, waking with a start or a scream. For a blissful moment, I would feel the relief that came with knowing that it was all just a nightmare. But then I would realize it wasn't a bad dream, it was a memory, the kind of memory I might never be able to erase.

My grandmother arrived the week before Christmas, armed with Marshall Field's shopping bags full of gifts and the tins of the foods we most associated with her: crybaby cookies for my father, fluffy tapioca pudding for my siblings and me, and fresh oysters from her butcher ("we must support the local businesses") for our traditional Christmas Eve stew. Grammie wasn't a cook or a baker; she made it clear that she had too busy a life to spend much time in the kitchen. But when she chose to make something, she did it lovingly and well.

All my life, my grandmother and I had been extraordinarily close. She was widowed, or "single," as my sister and I preferred to call her. She visited us so often that she was like a sixth member of our nuclear family, sleeping in the twin bed in my childhood room and talking to me late into the night about the life she had lived, and was still living, and all that was in store for me. As a young girl, I often stayed at her home on the North Shore of Chicago, spending summers immersed in her life of books and piano playing and "best girlfriends," as she called the community of women we joined for picnics at Ravinia, the summer home of the Chicago Symphony Orchestra.

Grammie believed in many things: good posture, three hours of piano practice a day, the evils of "big box" stores, the restorative power of a good book. I suspect that she wanted me to believe in these things, too. But she would never have told me so. She considered beginning a sentence with "I think you should" both bad strategy and bad form. Instead, she dispensed wisdom so effortlessly and unobtrusively that you were never certain she believed it to be wisdom at all. She presented her suggestions the way a health-conscious mother sneaks pureed spinach into the brownie recipe: in small doses, undetectable, usually in the company of a delicious story.

Late in the afternoon on the day before Christmas Eve, I sat listlessly wrapping gifts at our kitchen table. I can't recall if it was dark out yet, but in my memory the sun never shone during the Christmas of 1990—and in an odd way, I didn't want it to. The frenetic energy of the holidays had temporarily vacated our home. Everyone else was last-minute shopping, so only my grandmother and our ancient black-and-white cocker spaniel, Miss Kelly, remained in the house.

Grammie came into the kitchen, made us each a cup of tea, and sat down beside me, putting a plate of crybabies between us. One of the things I loved best about my grandmother was her stillness. She was undistractable when she turned her attention to you; though the term was not yet in vogue, she would have found "multitasking" hopelessly rude. So I wrapped presents as we listened to Kelly's old-dog snoring, while the snow fell heavily and silently outside. Eventually Grammie placed her teacup gently in its saucer, sat up a bit straighter, and clasped her hands together. Even today I can still see her fingers, which worried a bit before they came together, as if in prayer. She then leaned forward and said softly, but very firmly, "Isn't it wonderful, my darling, that you have your work to get back to?"

I knew in that moment that she was there with me, but also back in time, thinking of her own darkest chapter. Almost a half-century earlier, she had watched helplessly as the husband she adored wasted away from cancer, making her an impossibly young widow. Her love for the grandfather I'd never known had always seemed outsized and idealized to me. I don't think she ever stopped mourning him. But when she spoke of the year that followed his death, she didn't talk about the grief but instead about the "getting on." When I would ask Grammie about losing her husband, she would always say that returning to her work as a music teacher and concert pianist had been her salvation—an enforced respite from mourning, a reason to get out of bed when she was having one of her "down days."

She had loved her life before my grandfather's death, and she refused to fall out of love with it afterward. She knew that a retreat from work, or life, might be the beginning of a collapse—that if she gave up on any one aspect of her world, its entire architecture might come crashing down, never to be rebuilt. So she chose to move forward.

She didn't say any of this as we sat looking at each other across the kitchen table. She was too careful, too self-abnegating, to compare her grief from years earlier to what I was experiencing as the victim of a violent crime. She wasn't there to talk about her past. She was there to gently remind me of all of the reasons I had to move forward. "Aren't we lucky?" she would often say, finishing her sentence with the thought of some way in which we were fortunate. It might be the scent of the lilacs wafting in from her backyard in spring, or the fact that she lived close enough to Lake Michigan to walk to Tower Beach, or the "awfully good dogs" our family had owned over the years. Gratitude defined her far more than grief did. She believed that in life bad things were inevitable and that sometimes the best way to get back to the good was to allow the machinery of life and work to carry you there.

I went back to my job in Washington two weeks later. During those early days, putting a public face on my private angst took some effort. It was a performance that started with a script: I imagined a woman who had lived through violence but emerged triumphant, and I pretended to be her. I didn't always succeed. During those first six months, I felt tired and overwhelmed, ineffectual at work and depressed in life. But I showed up. In a sense, I existed in two worlds. There was my private life where, to a very small community of people I trusted, I unleashed my hurt, fear, and every exhausting detail I could recall about being kidnapped and raped. And there was my public life, where I tried to live, as much as possible, as if such a thing had never happened at all.

"You were like a Goffman case study back then," my brother Bobby, a social scientist and one of my closest confidantes, once said to me. He was alluding to *The Presentation of Self in Everyday Life*, a book by sociologist Erving Goffman. Goffman posits that life is a performance made up of front-stage, backstage, and offstage expressions of self. Knowing what it is appropriate to share, and when, is critical to an emotionally and professionally rewarding life. I'd like to say that I was self-aware enough to have been strategically presenting an ideal self during that first year. But it wasn't strategy that guided me. It was survival.

Survival. It's a word I've never much liked. It feels small and limiting, as if barely hanging on could ever be enough. What I am interested in, and what almost every person I've met who has lived through sexual violence is interested in, is greater than that. We know that our lives will never be the same, but we refuse to believe they can no longer be good. The essential question for someone who has been a victim of violence is this: how do I get there—to the good part—from here?

The answers are as diverse as is the population of those who have lived through sexual violence. Ask survivors what was most helpful for them, and many will say exactly what you'd expect: leaning on a spouse or partner, turning to a rape crisis center, talking to a pastor or rabbi, keeping a journal. But others will answer that question in ways that are not so obvious—and may even be counterintuitive. I've met men and women who have waxed rhapsodic about the healing powers of taking an improv comedy class, getting a new dog, hot yoga, cold martinis, and bowling (yes, bowling).

I came of age at a time when there was a deep cultural belief in the power of long-term talk therapy as an antidote to the lingering consequences of trauma. And yet more than a few survivors of violence I know have eschewed traditional therapy and engaged in what experts have coined "repressive coping." One of these women is my close friend and mentor, Bette Cerf Hill. She is beautiful, accomplished, and in possession of the wisdom that comes with nearly eighty years of life. And she believes, deeply, in selective silence.

Bette says that she publicly identifies as a rape survivor because doing so is important for her emotional health, and a way to stand in solidarity with other women. But over fifty years after being raped, she still chooses not to speak about the violence she lived through in any great detail. "Going back to the event, stirring the embers of memory, that is just way too painful."

"My own experience would be to tell a survivor of sexual violence that it gets better over time and heals much like other wounds, slowly but surely," Bette says. "Get up, get dressed, comb your hair, and go out into the street. Tell your friends and family. Treat it like a bad car accident. Get help for the injured part, which includes your dignity and your sense of self-determination."

Alisa Roadcup is separated from Bette Cerf Hill by two generations, but her experience has taught her largely the same thing. "During the first few years after I was sexually assaulted, I lived in various states of denial," Alisa says. "I used to judge this period harshly, wishing that I had it more together, sooner. But now I see that denial was a respite as I started to heal."

Bette Cerf Hill

For Alisa, healing herself has been linked to helping others. Her work with refugee girls through Heshima Kenya, a nonprofit organization in Nairobi, is an expression of that. "My experience with sexual violence broke my heart, and then it opened it," Alisa says. "It took time, and talking to those I trusted, but I was able to integrate my experience as a survivor into the broader narrative of who I was."

We are more resilient than we think we are, or than the world believes we can be, says Columbia University researcher George Bonanno. He has spent decades applying scientific methods to the study of grief and trauma, including the trauma of childhood sexual violence. "Most people just plain cope well," Bonanno says, noting that both the passage of time and what he calls "hardiness"—having a purpose in life, believing that you can learn from both good and bad experiences, and seeking support from family and friends—play key roles in rebuilding a life in the wake of trauma. Bonanno gets bonus points for arguing that "coping ugly"—railing at the incompetent emergency room doctor who performs your sexual assault exam, expressing anger at the family member who responds to your rape by

Alisa Roadcup

saying that "everything happens for a reason"—can actually do some very lovely things for the psyche.

Bonnano's findings are first-world focused, and for all of his optimism, his research still points to the fact that many survivors will need professional intervention and support as they work to rebuild their lives. This is just one of the reasons that our national network of rape crisis centers remains so vital. Still, his findings reinforce something I have seen again and again during a decade spent listening to survivors of sexual violence: resiliency is the rule, not the exception.

Recently, a woman I was interviewing turned the tables on me, asking what most helped me rebuild my life after rape. In response, I talked about my belief in the power of work, my activism on issues effecting women and girls, the benefits of the occasional second glass of chardonnay, and the healing power of rock 'n roll (I challenge anyone not to feel better after playing Nirvana's "Come As You Are" at maximum volume while driving on the George Washington Memorial Parkway). I liked the story that this answer told about me—that in grief, I was independent and ambitious, occasionally buzzed, and usually cool. And it was true, as far as it went.

But the full truth is more complicated, as full truths usually are. Because during the first year after I was attacked, and for more than a few years after that, I too, was transformed by talk. My then-partner, Clifton—a man who remains a close friend—was the person in whom I most often confided. Clifton is many things, but more than anything, he is an extraordinary listener, someone who believes that his silence will create a space for your words. He had driven through the night to be with me in the hospital after I was attacked and stayed with me nearly every day for a month afterward. When I began to talk—slowly at first, and then in a rush of graphic images and brutal details—he was the person I wanted to share my story with. I remember very little about what I said to him during those first six months, but I do recall how repetitive I was. My specialty was to talk endlessly about an aspect of my experience, assign meaning to it, and then talk about it all over again, just in case some fresh insight might alter my feelings about what had happened. Has anyone ever been more redundant in grief than I was?

My need to talk might arise at any hour (thankfully, Clifton was a night person). It might be prompted by my hearing, in some new way, David Bowie's "Rock 'n Roll Suicide," or seeing the film *Gorillas in the Mist*. I wept over more bad Hallmark commercials than a person with a fine-tuned sense of irony would ever care to admit—and I needed to talk about that, too. The merciful thing is that, over time, the hot breath of memory began to cool, and I needed less talk and more life. But the life part? I suspect that it was made possible, at least in part, by all of that talking.

I am certain of very little, but one thing is clear to me: being truly heard will change your life. Which means that someone has to do the listening. In her great novel about the female experience, *The House of Mirth*, Edith Wharton wrote of a "silence which is not solitude, but compassion holding its breath." We don't much believe in that type of silence anymore. In our social media-driven world, we are encouraged to endlessly, thoughtlessly, express (or post or tweet) every thought. And certainly, for survivors of sexual violence, speaking out, when we're so often told to remain quiet, can be a very good thing.

But what if the world turns less on what we say and more on what we have the courage to hear? It's a hard thing to listen—truly listen—to another person. It often means getting so close to their suffering that it breaks our own hearts. But inside our open, broken hearts—that's where compassion lies.

I suspect that the trick with trauma is to remain simultaneously close to it and far from it, keeping our memories near enough to inform our ability to care for others, but far enough away that we can go on living our beautiful, brutal, complicated lives.

Sasha Walters (right) with her sister Kim

Unbreakable: **Sasha Walters**

Sasha Walters is sitting across from me at a YWCA-organized gathering of activists, advocates, and philanthropists working on women's issues. She is wearing pink. She is wearing a headband. She is sitting up very straight. In my mind's eye, and in a flash, I typecast her.

And then, a few minutes into our group discussion, someone says something that makes Sasha laugh. Hers is not a large laugh, but it is an exuberant and unselfconscious one, and as she throws her head back, I see her tongue. Which is pierced. And this is the first time—though it will not be the last time—that I realize that Sasha Walters is kind of, sort of, but not quite the person I imagined she would be.

She was born in Alexandria, Virginia, an "army brat" who lived in three states and Korea before she was five years old. When Sasha's father left the service, the Walters family settled in Jacksonville, Illinois—a small town best known for its correctional facility and the Capitol Records plant that pressed many of the earliest Beatles albums. "It was a small town and not a suburb," says Sasha. "In some ways, it was a sheltered existence; in other ways, not. But it was what I knew."

During a family vacation to a Wisconsin Dells resort, thirteen-year-old Sasha was raped by a boy who was staying with his family in a cabin on the same property. The day had started the way most vacation days do, at the resort pool, a mecca for teenagers desperate to find one another and lose their overbearing parents and irritating younger siblings. "God, I loved hanging out at the pool," Sasha says. "I mean, what teenager doesn't live for that?"

Sasha can conjure the hours before she was raped with the sort of tactile clarity that often accompanies our recall of the lead-up to a traumatic event: the blueness of the sky, the laughing and shouts at the overcrowded pool, the way that she could mute those sounds each time she dove under water. But mostly, she remembers the feeling of being thirteen years old—on the cusp of everything, knowing nothing, utterly unafraid.

Sasha had been swimming for a while when a sixteen-year-old boy she'd met at the resort game room a few days earlier stood at the edge of the pool and asked if she wanted to watch a movie at his parents' cabin. She looked up into the shadow he cast, and thought for the briefest of moments. Yes.

Inside the cabin Sasha felt, for the first time that day, a chill. It may have been the blast of air conditioning on her still-damp skin, or it may have been the beginnings of fear—even today, she's not sure. She remembers asking where the family was and feeling reassured when the boy said that they had gone out for food and would be right back. She carefully placed her beach towel at the edge of the bed in front of the TV and sat down. "I didn't want it to be wet for anyone else while we watched the movie," she says.

When the boy grabbed her and shoved her onto the bed, her first feeling was not fear, but confusion. "I knew nothing about sexual violence, or even consensual sex, for that matter," Sasha says. "I remember screaming, 'What are you doing,' but he didn't respond. He just started pulling down my swimsuit." Sasha began to fight back, and he hit her on the thigh. She fought harder, and he grabbed her shoulders and slammed her head against the headboard. She stopped fighting. "Once I stopped resisting, I think I just dissociated—I could not tell you how long the rape lasted, because in a way I wasn't there."

What brought Sasha back was a knock on the cabin door. It was another boy who was staying at the resort, armed with a six-pack and ready to hang out. During the brief exchange between those two boys, Sasha was able to pull on her swimsuit, grab her towel—"I have no idea why I needed that towel, but I did not want to leave it"—and shove her way out the door. She ran as fast as she could to her family cabin, went straight to the bathroom, and leapt into the shower. All she wanted in that moment was to be warm, and clean.

When Sasha got out of the shower, she remembers that "Ko-komo," a song by the Beach Boys released just weeks earlier, was playing on the radio. "I will never forget hearing that song at that moment," says Sasha. "I had never felt so alone, and the song just became seared in my memory." During the next year, "Kokomo" would go on to become a Grammy-nominated number-one hit in the United States. Each time it came on the radio—unexpectedly and often—Sasha would feel that pain and fear all over again.

Later that same day, as Sasha sat alone and in shock in her room, her mother came in to tell her that there was a boy at the door to see her. Sasha refused to come out—"I was just frozen, really"—and asked her mother to tell him to leave. "Instead, my mom told me to write down our address because this boy was leaving the next day and wanted to write to me. And the amazing thing is, I did what I was told."

Sasha loves her mother and realizes that her parents had no idea what had just happened to their daughter. But their "failure to see" still haunts her. "If my mom had asked me why I wouldn't leave my room, or what was going on that I was refusing to talk to the boy at the door, everything could have been different," says Sasha. Instead, her mother's response left Sasha feeling unseen, unsafe, and certain that she needed to remain quiet about what had happened.

Being raped was the through-line in Sasha's young life, the moment when everything changed. "I forever lost the girl that I was that day," she says. "I lost my childhood. I lost my innocence. I learned that rapists take what they want, even if they look like—or literally are—the boy next door. And I learned that a lot of people, even people you love, aren't seeing it."

Sasha started eighth grade a few weeks later. "I had always been a tomboy, but that year I started to develop to the point that boys were paying attention to me. Other girls would call me 'slut' and 'whore,' which hurt probably more than it should have. The verbal taunts were garden-variety bullying that had nothing to do with the fact I had been raped, because no one knew about that." But the slurs were an external expression of what Sasha had come to feel about herself: "I was dirty. I was what they were saying I was. I deserved to be hurt."

When she talks about her teenage years, Sasha describes a world in which the adults seemed largely ineffectual: ever present, but rarely aware. She thinks that this may be more commonplace, even today, than we think. "The teachers, your parents, they already expect you to be some sort of a weirdo freak, so whatever you do, it's just 'Well, that's teenagers.' After I was raped, I became withdrawn and then promiscuous, and I gravitated to abusive boys. I really lost my will to say no. But no one ever said, 'Hey, are you OK?' I so wish they had asked."

When Sasha finally did tell her parents, a year later, they were upset that she hadn't turned to them sooner. Sasha remembers her father initially wanting to press charges, but that went nowhere. Instead, they took Sasha to a local counseling center, which she says was "a total bust. My therapist was an older woman who seemed to know nothing about teenagers and even less about rape. What I remember feeling is, I am *so* in this alone."

What got Sasha through those first few years? She gives much of the credit to her younger sister Kim (with whom she is photographed). Kim was just four years old at the time that Sasha was raped, with no knowledge of what had happened. Yet Sasha says that her sister "instinctively sensed that something was wrong with me, which is pretty amazing when you think about it." Kim admired Sasha the way younger sisters often do. "But honestly, she just saw what everyone else was missing. She was there with love, hugs, support. I love all of my family, but on some of those really dark days, Kim got me through."

Life changed for Sasha at college. She enrolled at Northern Illinois University and was majoring in psychology when a volunteer opportunity at Sexual Assault and Abuse Services, a DeKalb-area crisis center, caught her eye. From the very first volunteer training session, Sasha's worldview began to shift.

"Hearing people talk about rape as a human rights issue, not just a thing that happens to women who make so-called bad choices, really opened my eyes," says Sasha. "I had not thought about rape as something systemic, or the fact that there were people fighting, dedicating their lives to ending it. And I had never thought about what it meant to be a feminist. Once I grasped that, I was just, 'Yeah, sign me up.'"

The things Sasha learned during her volunteer training also impacted her in more personal ways. "I remember learning that crying or saying 'this is not a good idea' during a rape were both ways of communicating 'no' without saying 'no,'" says Sasha. "That was so important for me, because I had never explicitly said 'no' when he raped me."

"I was twenty years old when I looked in the mirror and finally could say, 'You are whole,'" Sasha says. She pauses, laughs, and then corrects herself: "mostly whole." Around that same time, Sasha went to work as a victim advocate, ultimately making a career of helping other women who have survived rape. And she began speaking publicly about her own experience with violence. She talks about rape because openness keeps her healthy and sane. But speaking out is about something bigger. "Society keeps with the blaming, and survivors keep with the silence," says Sasha. "I don't want to fuel that cycle anymore."

One of Sasha's great gifts is her Midwestern good-girl demeanor. In her role as a rape victim advocate, she speaks to community groups about concepts that they may not have considered: how often rape occurs, how poorly we protect our children, what needs to change, and what her audience needs to do to make that change happen. She is unintimidating, charming, and self-effacing—so good at challenging the status quo that the audience often does not feel challenged at all. When advocating for victims—a job that takes her into police precincts, state's attorneys' offices, and courtrooms—Sasha is invariably cheerful and polite. "I like people, and I want to give people the chance to do the right thing," she says.

Yet when those in power can't, or won't, respond with compassion or action, she can turn on a dime. Sasha Walters is easy to underestimate when you meet her, but it is impossible to underestimate her once you've been on the receiving end of her ire.

Today Sasha is married to her longtime partner, Ben, and she has a young daughter, Sophia. She says that she "loves, loves, loves" being a parent, and that her own experience informs her approach to motherhood. "I know my parents always loved me, but there was a lot that was missed," Sasha says. "Parents say, 'I want my kids to be able to tell me everything,' but honestly, that's not enough for me. I want to be aware of the things that my daughter might not be ready to tell me."

Sasha's relationship to her history is complicated. She believes that the sexual violence she survived informs much of what is good in her: her engagement in the anti-rape movement, her desire to be a good mother, her "crazy" belief that she can make the world a kinder, gentler place. "I love who I am now. I love my life. Would I be all of this without what happened to me? Who knows?"

Every now and then, Sasha still hears "Kokomo" on the radio. It's a cruel twist on the "Proust-bites-into-a-madeline" moment, the way that something as benign as a summer hit can cue years-old memories of trauma and grief. But Sasha doesn't fight her memories anymore. Sometimes, she'll even follow them. When she does, what she sees breaks her heart but also makes her proud: a thirteen-year-old girl standing in her family's vacation cabin bathroom, freshly showered, washed in grief, unaware of what a force she will one day be.

The Good Man: **Roger Canaff**

In "Let Us Now Praise Infamous Men," Joshua Ferris's very smart (and rather depressing) 2013 *New York Times Style Magazine* essay about the "steady decline" of the male hero, Ferris makes the convincing argument that the men we culturally admire aren't what they used to be.

Once we worshipped at the altar of truth (Albert Einstein), justice (Nelson Mandela), and quiet courage (Jackie Robinson). Today, the men who capture our collective imagination are made of what Ferris calls "darker stuff." What unites the Kanye Wests and Mark Zuckerbergs of the word—two of the men Ferris name-checks in his critique—are raw talent, outsized drive, and the ability to make an impact. But the old-school idea of the "good man"? It seems to have gone the way of the BlackBerry. Humility? That's for losers. Earnestness? It was kicked to the curb by *Seinfeld*, sometime in the early nineties. Social responsibility? If it matters at all, it's as a hobby to be picked up—like tennis or squash—after you're rich, famous, and ready to "give back."

All of which is to say that Roger Canaff is a very old-school man. He is not an icon—if he were one, I suspect that he would reject the label—but a gifted prosecutor and victim advocate. A former assistant attorney general for the state of New York, Roger spent over a decade successfully prosecuting cases involving sexual abuse, child abuse, and elder abuse. It has never been easy work. But it is work that he clearly loves.

Roger is the kind of prosecutor who says things like, "We're in this to do the right thing," and is so obviously sincere that he avoids (just barely) sounding like a character on Lifetime TV. If he has a point to make in meetings—particularly one that he is especially certain about—he often prefaces his statement with, "I may be wrong about this, but. . . ." When he parts company with friends, he sometimes says good-bye, but more often says, "Take care."

Roger is as aware as the victim advocates and social workers he works closely with that he often benefits from what is sometimes called "white male privilege." When he is distrusted because of this, he understands why. "Look, I am the first to say it: the world still genuflects far too much to men," Roger says. "And that can be especially true in the law and order world. So when a victim advocate isn't sure I 'get it' about rape because I'm a man, it's not personal. I'm just a symbol."

Symbolism is at the heart of Roger's decision to come out as a survivor of childhood sexual violence. He believes in the power of survivor stories, the ways that the issue is made real when the world encounters a woman or man who has been abused. But mostly, he believes that it's his turn.

"Time and time again, I have watched rape victims come forward, sometimes at great risk to themselves," Roger says. "I won cases because they were willing to say, 'Yes, rape happened.' How could I claim to speak for victims as a prosecutor when I didn't have the courage to acknowledge that I had also been abused?"

Roger was five years old when he was first raped by a trusted babysitter, a teenage boy who lived in the Canaff family's Loudoun County, Virginia, neighborhood. "The perpetrator, that babysitter, was literally the boy next door," Roger says. "My parents were just good, trusting people who would never have conceived of the idea that a neighborhood kid could do so much harm."

The abuse continued for four years. At the time that it was happening—which it did on almost every occasion when the babysitter was called on by Roger's unsuspecting parents—Roger says that he emotionally went numb. "I experienced physical pain," Roger recalls. "But I accepted it, the way that young kids who are told by someone they trust that something is okay will."

The abuse ended when Roger was nine and his parents moved on to another babysitter, with no awareness of what had been done to their son. "I did not reflect on it, I did not talk about it—I just sort of integrated it into my life."

But being abused left its mark on Roger, in ways that took him years—and some "really good therapy"—to understand. "There was a sadness about me that started during that time, and it never really left," Roger says. "Kids hide sadness with whatever they've got—attitude, bullying, laziness—and I was really good at hiding mine in a dozen screwed-up ways."

Roger recalls his adolescence as a time when he was at war with himself, a small-town kid acting out for a community of people who weren't noticing him much at all. He gained weight—Roger thinks it may have been a form of self-protection—and lost his ability to trust.

In the tenth grade, a sympathetic high school track coach encouraged Roger to join the track team. Did finding a sport he was good at change his life, *Friday Night Lights*-style? "Are you kidding me?" Roger laughs. "I sucked. But I lost fifty pounds, figured out how to dress, and got a little more confident with girls."

Roger says that he has always been a control freak. "If my friends and I were driving somewhere and we didn't have directions, if I lost a wallet or left my backpack at school, I would freak out, beyond what was normal," he recalls. It was classic "victim behavior"—clinging tightly to control after being rendered so powerless for so long. But at the time, Roger just thought of himself as "quirky, and not in a good way."

Roger's control issues turned out to be a blessing in disguise, if only because explaining his behavior became the impetus for his disclosing, at the age of nineteen, that he had been raped as a child. "I felt, for lack of a better word, that I was 'entitled' to explain why I had these freak-outs, at least to my closest friends," Roger says. "By late high school, I had a really great group of guys I trusted—we are all still close friends today—and I decided to exercise that trust."

Roger's friend Clem was the first person he talked to. Roger can't recall the exact words he used to describe being raped as a child. But he remembers Clem's compassionate response as if it happened last week. "Clem knew nothing about helping someone who had survived sexual violence," Roger says. "I mean, he was a kid like I was—we were nineteen years old."

But in some fundamental way, Clem's response taught Roger everything he would later need to know about working with victims. "He told me that he was sorry for what I had gone through," Roger says. "He let me know that he was there for me, and didn't judge or blame. And he listened in a way that told me that he really *wanted* to hear what I was saying."

Around that same time, Roger shared his story with his Uncle Richard, one of a handful of trusted adults in his life. "I could feel that my story actually hurt him," Roger says, "which somehow helped. You know, that idea that you can feel someone else's pain is pretty powerful stuff."

The next day Richard bought Roger *Victims No Longer*, one of the first books written for men healing from child sexual abuse. Roger says that the gesture meant almost as much to him as the book did. It was his uncle's way of acknowledging that something serious and real had happened—and that Roger needed to take care of himself.

Roger chose at the time—it was 1985—not to tell his parents that he had been abused. He was certain they would blame themselves, and when he finally disclosed his story to them, in 2012, he was proven right. The anguish they experienced in learning what had happened to their son so many years ago was, for Roger, the single most difficult aspect of going public as a rape survivor.

"Frankly, if I had not decided to come forward, I would have kept it from them for the rest of their lives," he says. "They were blameless, good people who had no idea that something this bad could be happening in their home when they went out."

In the end, Roger weighed the pain he would inflict on his parents by sharing his story against the good he might do if he went public. He knows he made the right decision, but he is not unconflicted about it. "It's never just your story," he says. "I learned that while working as a prosecutor."

Law was, in many ways, a natural fit for Roger. From an early age, he loved to write and read (he says that John Steinbeck's *East of Eden* changed his life). Debating and public speaking also came naturally to him. Roger credits his father for this, at least in part. "My dad was a yellow-dog Democrat who loved to rant about politics," Roger says. "I like to think that my rants are a little more subtle, or at least esoteric—but just as heartfelt."

Roger attended the University of North Carolina at Chapel Hill as an undergraduate and became active in the North Carolina Student Legislature—"the best education possible in the heartache and hubris of politics"—before graduating from their Chapel Hill law school in 1995. His first job, as the assistant commonwealth's attorney in Alexandria, Virginia, brought him close to the nation's capital and a stone's throw away from his sister, who lived in Alexandria, and his parents, who still resided in the Loudoun County area.

Prosecuting his first child abuse case felt like coming home in another way. "In the twenty minutes it took to make my first closing argument to a jury in my first child sex abuse case, three years of studying and misery and law school loans were made worth it." Roger moved to New York a few years later and went to work as a special victims assistant district attorney in the Bronx.

As a lawyer, Roger considers his defining quality to be his passion. "Sit across the table from an elderly woman who has been raped, or watch a videotape of a child being physically abused by a parent they still clearly love, and if you are human, you are going to feel that deeply," Roger says. But paradoxically—or perhaps not—one of the things Roger seems most passionate about is the concept of "reason."

"You have got to be, for lack of a better word, 'cool,'" Roger says. "I did not—I do not—'hate' perpetrators. I was polite when I questioned them, polite to their attorneys, cordial to their families when they stood behind us in court. Because it's not your anger—or your need to express that—that this job is about. It's about that victim, and doing all that you can so it never happens to anyone again."

All of this begs the inevitable question of whether Roger gravitated to these cases because he was a victim himself. His answer is a (very qualified) yes.

"It would be foolish to assume that the abuse had no effect on my choice to become a prosecutor. Especially because I've worked largely on sex crimes and child abuse cases, issues very close to home."

But choice is a complicated concept. "My parents were social justice-oriented Catholics, and my sister and I were raised to do something meaningful with our lives," Roger says. "So there was also that factor. And this was the area I understood in a real-world way, which made it an area where I might make a difference professionally."

Roger pauses, thinks about his history of cases, and says, "The one thing I am absolutely certain of is that I never saw myself in the chair"—"the chair" being prosecutor-speak for the victim on the witness stand.

The magnetic field for Roger as a prosecutor may be less the issue of sexual abuse and more a desire to be close to what he believes is real. "People have an almost primal need to distance themselves from horror," Roger says. "You see that as a prosecutor. Hell, it's why a jury will acquit in a rape case that unnerves them—they convince themselves that if what this victim says occurred is bad enough, *it must not have happened.*

"My own experience as a victim showed me, at a very early age, that sometimes the bad stuff—the stuff people want to look away from—is the true stuff," Roger says. "And it is inarguable that I gravitate to truth."

Roger considers himself a good lawyer, not a great one. "There are star prosecutors who are much better at thinking on their feet or wowing a courtroom," he says. "But, and I hope this doesn't sound arrogant, I was great in one area: working with victims. Largely, I think, because they felt my empathy. Was that true because of what I went through? I genuinely don't know," Roger says. "Is it a gift for a prosecutor to feel that connection with a victim? Absolutely."

I ask Roger if he ever shared the fact that he is a survivor with his fellow prosecutors. By way of an answer, he tells me the story of an assistant district attorney he worked with in the Bronx DA's office. She was a few years older than Roger—he was about thirty at the time—and smart, capable, and committed. "I respected her, and I never doubted that she was on the side of the good," Roger says.

One day, Roger stopped by her office as she was finishing up a meeting with the young man at the center of a child sex abuse case she had successfully prosecuted (the abuse had occurred years earlier). After she gave the man a warm hug good-bye, she turned to Roger, who congratulated her on her victory. "It's great, and he's doing really well," Roger remembers her responding. She then frowned, paused, and said, "It's kind of weird though. He just told me he wants to be a schoolteacher."

Roger recalls that comment with the clarity that often accompanies the moment when sexual violence survivors realize that their instinct to remain silent exists for a reason. For Roger, his colleague's comment was the lifting of a veil, a reminder that stereotypes about male childhood sexual violence victims were potent and prevalent, even in quarters where we might imagine they don't exist at all.

"I think that I said something like, 'You know, that's a myth,' or 'There's no evidence that shows that men who were raped as children will be a danger to children later on,'" Roger recalls. "What I really wanted to say was, 'Wow, you don't get it. And if you're prosecuting these cases, you damn well should.'"

Roger decided—"almost literally in that moment"—that for as long as he remained active in sex crimes prosecution, he would not share his personal story in any public forum. "Not because I was ashamed," Roger says. "Because I was realistic. At that time, it would have changed the way I was seen as a lawyer, and that would have affected my ability to prosecute cases. Which was not an option."

When I mention that his colleague will likely read this profile at some point, Roger responds with a nod and a slight smile: "Good." He then clarifies what he means. "You know, she may not recognize herself in that story. The optimist in me hopes that if she doesn't, it's because she's become much better educated over all of these years. But the realist in me knows that there are still a lot of stereotypes in circulation about male rape victims."

It has proven difficult for our culture to confront the scope and scale of rape and abuse in general—and addressing sexual violence against men and boys has been especially challenging. Sexual abuse has been seen historically as a women's issue. Rape-prevention campaigns have largely focused on men as perpetrators and women as victims. Crisis centers and victim resources are often developed for, and by, women.

But there is a growing awareness, spurred on by a series of high-profile abuse cases—including former Penn State coach Jerry Sandusky's conviction on child molestation charges, and the ongoing international scandal of sexual violence in the Catholic Church—that there are more men like Roger than most people realize. As is usually the case, the data that supports this has existed for far longer than our public awareness. A 2005 study conducted by the Centers for Disease Control estimated that 16 percent of American males were sexually abused by the age of eighteen.

David Lisak, a researcher and the founder of 1in6, a national non-profit focused on male sexual violence victims, says that the stories of men like Roger are critical to changing the conversation, creating a series of "aha" moments that are calling into question many of our notions about who has survived abuse. "The community of sexual violence survivors is larger and more diverse than we previously acknowledged," Lisak says. "That's why hearing from male survivors is game changing. It challenges the public to look at everything—who's been abused, how we help them, how big the problem is—in a different way."

Today, Roger is retired from the New York state's attorney's office. He serves as an in-demand public speaker and trains first responders—police officers, EMTs, fellow prosecutors—on how best to work with victims and prosecute cases in the criminal courts. He blogs on the high-profile cases involving sexual assault that our 24/7 news networks fixate on, and on smaller stories that he believes the world needs to know about.

He is still "passionate"—his word, again—about the law. "You know, when it works, it's a beautiful thing," Roger says. "There's a moment when everything comes together—the evidence, the victim testimony, the hearts of the jurors. When you are that prosecutor, and you get to go home that night and say, 'The world is a little safer, and a victim was believed,' that's a great day's work. It just doesn't happen enough."

Roger feels, increasingly, the law's limitations. Forty years after the advent of the rape crisis movement—after decades of significant legal reform—criminal justice rates for rape victims remain static. Victim blaming has become more, and not less, commonplace in the courtroom and in the court of public opinion. With alarming frequency, prosecutors are declining to take on non-stranger rape cases. "The excuse is, 'I believe you, but I can't win that one—we can't prove it; it's he says, she says,'" Roger says. "It sounds logical, but it's the reason rapists and child abusers get the chance to become serial offenders."

Roger believes that the media is critical to changing much of that. "So much of what jurors and judges feel about rape has been learned long before they enter that courtroom," Roger says. "It's about social media, about TV and film, about music and books. Some of it's good. A lot of it isn't. For me, talking to the public and not just in the courtroom is the solution."

So wherever he goes, Roger is talking. And, when he needs to, arguing (ever civilly, of course). "In a way, I'm still prosecuting cases," Roger says. "I'm just trying to do it in front of a different sort of jury. Because we have to see the public as exactly that—people who need to hear these stories and be convinced."

One of the things I have long admired about Roger is his ambition. He is greedy with it—in the best way possible—and the things that he wants never seem small. *Total change, transformation, a completely new way* are all phrases I've heard him use. Which is why, when we talk about what he hopes his story might mean once it's published in this book, I'm surprised by the simplicity—the touching simplicity—of his desire.

"If some kid who is struggling sees my story and says, 'Hey, that guy made it through, so maybe I can, too,' that would be pretty fantastic," Roger says. "If it's more than one kid, I'll feel damn good about that, too."

The Realist: **Nobuko Nagaoka**

She dislikes me instantly and, to my mind at least, irrationally.

We were introduced when I was in my twenties and she in her early thirties. I had just accepted a job at Leo Burnett, a Chicago-based advertising agency. Nobuko was known in the agency as an immensely talented, immensely mercurial art director. I was one of the creative department's newest copywriters, with no experience of my own with which to judge her talent or temperament.

One of the agency's creative directors had the inspired idea of pairing us together to work on a new advertising campaign. "She's difficult and, well, you're not—so we think this might work," he said. Well, thanks—I guess. Later that day, after Nobuko and I had been introduced, that same creative director stopped me in the lobby to report back on the impression I'd made. "It didn't go badly. She says she thinks you might have 'a silver spoon up your ass.' But she wants to work with you."

If I am to be insulted, I prefer that the idiom used at least be accurate, but no matter—Nobuko and I were thrust into a professional partnership. Over time, I would see that her initial response to me was pure Nobuko. She is quick to judge, fundamentally distrusting, and always ready to combine two clichés into one brilliant insult. But when she realizes that she has been wrong about someone, no one is more willing than Nobuko to say so.

In my case, that realization came slowly. "You are a hard-working princess," she said to me a few weeks and many late nights after we started working together. Her comment represented a kind of progress: she was moving from conflated idioms to halfhearted compliments.

The real breakthrough occurred several months into our relationship, when Nobuko and I were putting in yet another late night at a downtown Chicago studio. It was 2:00 a.m. when she summoned a junior account executive to announce—Nobuko does not ask, she announces—that he needed to walk us to the cabstand on Wacker Drive. When he had left the room to let us finish up, she turned, looked me in the eyes, and said, "This is going to be hard for someone *like you* to understand, but I was raped when I first came to America, and now I am very careful when I leave buildings at night."

Of course, I did understand, at least to some degree. And that night, as we shared our stories (and made that beleaguered account executive wait even longer before walking us out), Nobuko began to see me differently, I began to see her differently, and we set in motion a friendship that has become one of the constants of my adult life. It's a relationship forged on more than just a shared history of violence. We are also both dog lovers, we prefer vinyl LPs to digital downloads, and we share a similar interest in Modernism. But it was that first, long conversation about the violence we'd lived through that transformed our relationship.

Nobuko was born in Osaka, Japan, the daughter of a dentist father and a homemaker mother who were deeply invested in Japanese tradition. "They wanted me to marry and have a family. I could not be that. I was a disappointment in that way, I was always different, not a conformist."

She was, from a very early age, fascinated with America. "In Japan, everything is so orderly. There is no choice. If you don't say, do, or wear the right thing, you are an outcast. But America, what I saw in your films, here you have freedom. Growing up, I saw Americans as accepting and giving. This was the place where someone like me could have a shot."

By the time she was twenty, Nobuko's parents had largely given up on the idea of her marrying and had begun to pressure her to become a dentist like her father. "I would have been very bad at that, yes?" she says, and it's true—the idea of Nobuko with a dental drill is vaguely ominous.

So instead of a career in dentistry, she left for America. Speaking only Japanese, she enrolled in an English-as-a-second-language program at the University of Michigan in Ann Arbor and began to acclimate to the United States. "I think my parents finally saw that I would never be happy in Japan and just said to me, 'OK, you go now.' So I did. I never doubted this course; I knew I was meant to be here."

Nine months later, when she was taking a weekend trip to New York City—a place she had imagined visiting since she was young— she was apprehended in the elevator of a hotel and then raped. "I was so naïve," Nobuko says. "You know, it was all *Breakfast at Tiffany's* in my head, and then I check into a hotel where the man at the front desk has a baseball bat. Very stupid."

The man who raped Nobuko told her he was a Vietnam veteran. "The funny thing is that, in Japan, I had been really into all of those movies about American soldiers coming back ruined after going to Vietnam—*Coming Home*, *Apocalypse Now*, *The Deer Hunter*—so while he raped me, I decided that I did feel sorry for him . . . I refused to see myself as the victim. In my mind he became the victim. I looked at him and thought, 'It is you who are damaged, not me.' This helped. The rape was just one hour. I cannot let one hour of my life have that much effect on me."

"It was just one hour" is a phrase I have heard Nobuko use repeatedly over the years, like a mantra—or a wish. She prefers to see the rape she survived measured in time and not psychic impact. When I ask her about this, she pauses, thinks for a moment and then says, "Yes. Maybe it is denial, but I have always believed in minimizing it." Adds Nobuko, "If I didn't make it seem smaller, I might not have been able to go on with the work I had to do, like getting through school and getting a job."

Nobuko's feelings about her own experience are also shaped by a historical sense of sexual violence. "We did not talk about rape in my family, never. But I think I first learned of it in junior high when my father—who was interested in history—gave me a book called *The Rape of Nanking*, about rapes inflicted on the Chinese by the Imperial Japanese Army. It was a banned book in Japan at one time, but my father thought I should read it. After I was raped myself, I would think of that book and the horrible things that happened to those women and I would say, 'I am just lucky I am alive. This was not as bad as that. I cannot dwell.'"

Nobuko did not report the rape. She felt certain that her family would make her return to Japan if they knew about it. And as much as she loved America, she was equally certain that the American legal system could not help her. "Something I had read or seen, maybe in all of those American films, told me that rape victims were blamed here," Nobuko says. "Also, I was aware of the stereotype about Japanese women—the 'geisha girl,' you know. So I kept quiet. It was not useful crying over spilt milk."

Nobuko did tell her then-boyfriend, a fellow university student. "I did not make a big thing of it. I just casually said, 'Oh, in New York this happened.' I remember he was more upset than I was. But I focused on the fact that I survived the duration. I did not want to turn to anyone else for pity."

Nobuko did, however, turn to her journal. "I wrote about what had happened, what I felt, even what he had said to me while he raped me. I wanted those words recorded. I wanted to not be judged, and the journal could not judge. Of course, I barely spoke English at the time, so page after page in the journal is my writing in Japanese. Only the word 'rape' is in English."

Nobuko shows me that journal, and the visual effect is powerful. There is her elegant, lovely Japanese script—so beautiful to my American eyes that it is difficult to imagine the ugly story being told in those pages. But then there is the word "rape," popping up in English on page after page, a graphic reminder of the outsize role that this "one hour" played in her early life.

At the time she first showed me her journal, I was left with the impression that Nobuko had chosen to write the word "rape" in English because the Japanese term was not familiar to her. But many years later, she tells me that this was not the case.

"Of course I knew the word for 'rape' in Japanese," Nobuko says (still declining to speak it in Japanese). "But to write it down in my own language would have made what had happened real. If I used English, it was as if I was still protected. It did not feel so awful. In English, what happened to me felt less . . . icky."

I had never before heard Nobuko use the word "icky." She is fond of strong words, declarative words, even aggressive words, but never vague or girlish words. And with that "icky," I suddenly see her as a twenty-year-old girl, arriving in New York City, so in love with the idea of American freedom that she has not yet grasped the idea of American risk, walking with a single bag and all of that belief into a hotel in Manhattan.

And though I don't want to, I can also imagine her, an hour later—or maybe it was longer—walking back onto the streets of the city, clinging to what must have been a broken, or at least battered, American dream. And I love her for continuing to dream it.

"Women who have been raped, we have to work harder to move forward. But my philosophy is, 'This too can pass,'" says Nobuko. She has jumbled yet another idiom, replacing the "will" in the sentence with a "can." It's a subtle alternation of an overused phrase, and I like to think that it's Nobuko's way of acknowledging that for some of us, the trauma of rape doesn't just "pass." And I love her for seeing that, too.

A Low Hum:
Michelle Lugalia-Hollon

Michelle Lugalia-Hollon grew up in Ngumba Estate, a community located on the outskirts of Nairobi, Kenya. When she speaks of her childhood home, she describes a city teeming with energy. "It was rugged then, and everything seemed to be in motion," says Michelle. "There were no cemented roads, and there were plenty of open-air markets, stores, schools, and places for us to play. Noise, all the time. I suppose it could be described as chaotic—it *was* chaotic—but it was wonderful."

As she speaks of her Nairobi childhood, Michelle's words are sharply at odds with her own physicality. There is an elegant still-ness about her. Michelle gestures minimally, sometimes leaning in for emphasis, and then slowly leaning back once her point has been made. She seems to depend on the words themselves, and not ex-traneous flourishes, to convey her experiences. As she confides the details of being sexually assaulted—which she does candidly and at great length—there remains something intensely private about her. She speaks carefully, lingering over the most painful words, as if stay-ing with them might rob them of their power.

Michelle was eight years old when a much older cousin sexually assaulted her. "My brother and I looked up to him, we thought of him as very 'cool,'" says Michelle. "He would find me whenever I was alone and abused me on many occasions. I was confused, not sure what to do. I had no language for what was happening, and I felt such shame. I could not say a word to my father."

"My family is very close, but we value independence," says Mi-chelle. "Perhaps this is something Kenyan about us, but we keep to ourselves what we feel would hurt others or would venture us into a difficult conversation."

I ask Michelle if such an emphasis on silence and self-sufficiency made things more difficult for her growing up, and she hesitates. "Before I was molested, I would say that I was not troubled by it," Michelle says. "My mother died when I was very young and my brother, father, and I had the fiercest love for each other, one that did not need words. We tried to solve our own problems, particularly those that carried a lot of emotional weight. Later, all of this silence made it hard for me to speak about my cousin."

One of Michelle's greatest fears was that she might become pregnant as a result of the sexual assaults. "I was beginning to enter puberty, and my body began to change," Michelle recalls. "Out of youthful ignorance, I really believed that I might be carrying a child, though this was not possible. If I were pregnant, my father would have to kick me out of the house, or I would have to run away in order to spare our family any shame. As I said, I come from a very loving family, but at that time in Kenya, young girls who became pregnant were abandoned or would run away."

Four years later, Michelle's family moved to America—Houston, Texas—where for the first time she heard someone speak publicly about sexual violence. "It was at our church, where a woman came forward to tell her story of having been raped," Michelle recalls. "I was emboldened by that, and I told my best friend about what had happened to me. She was also Kenyan, which felt safe, and we were in America, which made things seem different. My friend expressed sympathy, and that helped me. But I was still afraid to speak out beyond that."

Women's health and welfare had always interested Michelle, so she decided to study public health at school, ultimately receiving her master's from Harvard University. It was during her undergraduate and graduate classes that she began to look at the violence she had lived through as not only a women's rights issue, but as part of a broader public health crisis. "Rape and sexual violence cost victims and communities so much—emotionally, economically, and socially. And because I lived that before I studied it, this was very real to me. But it took me years to find a way to voice that in a personal way."

Michelle's real turning point came when she attended Speak-OUT, a campus anti-rape program where students who had lived through sexual violence were invited to share their stories. "At first I had no intention of sharing. But as I listened, some part of me wanted to become one of the strong women sharing their stories. I wanted to hear my story out loud; I was curious how I would feel afterwards, curious about how it would sound and whether it would become real. And when I went up to speak and heard my own words, I knew that it would always be real after that."

It is the absence of language, not language itself, that most often accompanies sexual violence. "All truth is good, but not all truth is good to say," says the well-worn African proverb, and Michelle's silence over the years was consistent with such a belief. Yet the reality of violence was ever-present for her. "The abuse I lived through became background music to my life, in the sense that I would live my life, but the reality of it was always present," says Michelle. "Like an underlying hum."

When Michelle looks back on her silence in the wake of childhood sexual abuse, she articulates a single, clear regret. "The thing I am most sorry about is that I underestimated my father's love, his sense of justice, and his ability to support me," Michelle says. "I should have trusted him and myself enough to tell him. I shouldn't have had to carry this all these years. Keeping it to myself and keeping it from my father, who loves me, just prolonged my suffering."

I ask Michelle when she finally was able to tell her father, and she looks at me with surprise. "I have still never told him," she says.

The Heartbreaker:
Dorothy Allison

Her mother told her to write funny stories, because funny is what people want—and need—to hear. And novelist Dorothy Allison is nothing if not a woman who believes in listening to her mother.

So she tells stories on the page, and in life, that are clever and charming and darkly hilarious. Not since Flannery O'Connor, one of Dorothy's literary heroes and a writer to whom she is frequently compared, has an author captured the rural South with such a quick wit and slow drawl. "Like as not, the worst moments in your life were followed by a moment when you were just drunk with the joy of being alive," she says. "Lord help you if you don't take that laughter when you can."

Those "worst moments" have been many in Dorothy Allison's life, and she writes about what she knows: extreme poverty, discrimination, casual violence, childhood sexual abuse. She crafts stories that are "mean" and "dangerous" and "forbidden," three words she uses often and with relish. On the page, as in person, Dorothy can shift from heartbreak to humor on a dime. But she doesn't do shock for shock's sake. She is too wise and too literarily ambitious for that. Her stories are shocking because life, when observed carefully, often *is* shocking.

Dorothy calls herself "an outlaw," revels in a past that is as wild as one might expect from a woman who made her way to New York City during the Studio 54 era and collects black leather jackets (preferably of the rhinestone cowboy variety). Though she was raised on gospel music, the soundtrack of the Deep South, her great musical love is rock 'n roll. She grew up wanting to be Janis Joplin but tells me that watching a "gorgeous" Jim Morrison of the Doors perform in his trademark leather pants confirmed for her that she was a lesbian (it may also explain her electrifying performances at book readings). Does she take pleasure in the fact that she has been dubbed a literary rock star? Yes.

It is undeniable that Dorothy Allison is a bold woman. But about her there is also the faint whiff of the good girl she has always been. She is hardworking and unselfishly cause-oriented—she was fighting for a woman's right to day care long before she imagined having a child of her own. She loves her partner of twenty-five years, musician Alix Layman, and speaks proudly of the life that they've built in Northern California with their son, Wolf Michael. When she expounds on a subject that she cares deeply about—and there are many—she can be righteous, but rarely self-righteous. "I come from a Christ-haunted culture," she shrugs, alluding to Flannery O'Connor's famous description of the Southern ethos.

I discovered Dorothy Allison's writing in early 1992, when her first novel, *Bastard Out of Carolina*, was just beginning to receive praise (the book would go on to be nominated for a National Book Award). A close friend, who was getting his doctorate in English literature at the time, recommended *Bastard* to me with an enthusiasm that was rare for him. Seventeen years later, when I tell Dorothy this, she laughs—guffaws, to be more accurate—and says, "Goddamn! When they started praising me at Yale and Haaaahvard, I thought I must have messed up something awful."

Bastard Out of Carolina is fiction grounded in deeply personal fact. Like Bone Cartwright, the book's indelible young protagonist, Dorothy was born in 1949 to a poor, unmarried, fifteen year old who dropped out of the seventh grade to work as a waitress to support herself and her first child. Like Bone, Dorothy grew up in Greenville County, South Carolina, a member of an extended family that she describes as loving, large, and only sporadically law-abiding. They were poor, but they refused to be noble. And like Bone, Dorothy lived through eight years of physical and sexual violence at the hands of a stepfather her mother could not, or would not—and even today, Dorothy never seems quite sure which—leave.

Bone is the novel's main character and its camera, the eyes through which Dorothy asks readers to see the sexual and domestic violence that the world often ignores. She is a hero whom Dorothy had the courage to write as a victim—the type of person rarely seen in popular culture, but not so difficult to find in real life. Bone is broken by her stepfather's abuse, but remains unbowed. She is hilarious, she is loving, and she is deeply angry—sometimes by turns, sometimes all at once. This is someone we want, if not to *be*, at least to *be like*. Someone very much like Dorothy.

This was, of course, by design. In the afterward to the twentieth-anniversary edition of *Bastard*, published in 2012, Dorothy writes that she wanted Bone to be her own "best self . . . unafraid, stubborn, resilient, and capable of enormous compassion." Yet Dorothy is clear about the differences between her fictional alter ego and the child she once was. "I wrote the story of a girl that faces down a monster, that's true," says Dorothy. "And I went through a lot of what Bone went through. But I was never as brave as Bone," she sighs. "I wanted to be. But I wasn't."

Dorothy was five years old when her stepfather, a failed route salesman with an anger management problem, first abused her as they sat in a hospital parking lot while her mother miscarried inside. Dorothy was too scared and ashamed to tell anyone what had happened. Over the next eight years, the sexual and physical abuse continued and escalated. Safety—to the degree that it existed at all in Dorothy's home—was only secured through a set of desperate, ongoing negotiations.

"My mama would do what she could to distract my stepfather out of his rages so that he wouldn't beat us so brutally," says Dorothy. "My younger sisters and I loved each other, but we would fight over who would have to sleep closest to the door—because the one closest to the door might be the one he came for at night. I will spend a lifetime trying to make sense of that, to forgive myself for that mean compromise, for putting someone I love in harm's way."

Dorothy believes that her mother did not know the extent of the abuse that was occurring in their home, yet over time, her mother's illusions could not have been easy to cling to. When Dorothy was eight, she was beaten so badly that it caused a "family scandal." Her mother packed up her girls and left for a motel, but supporting herself and her three daughters on a waitress's salary proved impossible, so when the money ran out two weeks later, they returned home.

At eleven, Dorothy told one of her cousins that her stepfather was sexually abusing her, and the cousin went to Dorothy's mother. Again they left. But Dorothy's stepfather promised her mother that he would change, and with little money and fewer options—there were no shelter services available—they went back.

Dorothy remembers little of the first two years that followed that second return home.

Later, when her stepfather was medicated for his anger, he became easier to avoid, and Dorothy and her sisters found new ways to conspire to stay clear of him. Still, reflecting today on her final years at home, Dorothy says that she "barely made it out."

To understand how Dorothy did escape is to understand the power of *the story*. Not the award-winning stories that Dorothy Allison, the novelist, would one day write, but the stories that Dorothy Allison, the young girl, told herself so that she could live. "Look at your life as a story, and revise it," Dorothy tells me. "Write yourself a new ending. Because you don't have to be what they tell you you are going to be."

It's not as simple as that, of course, and no one knows this better than Dorothy. She describes the race- and class-bound South Carolina she came of age in as a "medieval empire"—a brutal environment for a young, desperately poor, and not–yet–out lesbian girl whose family was held in communal contempt. In Dorothy's hometown, the conditions in which the working poor were born were almost always the conditions in which they died (if they were fortunate enough not to fall farther down on the class ladder). No member of Dorothy's family—immediate or extended—had ever graduated from twelfth grade. "My uncles went to jail like other boys go to high school," Dorothy has written.

Dorothy's own escape from poverty was greased by extraordinary intelligence and an unwavering belief. She was smart, but more importantly, she believed herself to be smart. "That was all mama," she says. "I wrote a lot of stuff when I was little—there was one play I wrote, based on a bad Disney movie, and my mama just loved that play. She was convinced that I was truly a genius. Well, it's a damn good thing when your mama thinks you are a genius. She told me I would be someone until it became true."

Dorothy says her mother taught her something else: the art of performance. Ruth Anne Gibson spent forty years as a waitress, and Dorothy describes a mother in possession of a charm that can be the last, desperate defense of an impoverished woman. "Mama taught me how to turn misery into something people might sympathize with, might want to help. She used a smile to tease extra time out of bill collectors more often than I care to remember. It was theater, plain and simple."

"The people who have money to give, the ladies from the Junior League, they choose 'a worthy,'" says Dorothy. "So you get good grades, you are polite, you use good diction. And when you get that scholarship, you run like hell."

Dorothy attended Florida Presbyterian College on a National Merit Scholarship. "I could have gone to Michigan State, but I needed a coat—and I swear to you, I could not afford that coat." She majored in anthropology, an inspired choice for a girl who had spent much of her first eighteen years as an outsider looking in. It was the sixties, an era of self-discovery and self-reinvention, and Dorothy made the most of it. She embraced her sexuality, began to date women openly, played down her Southern accent, and put as much distance as she could between herself and her family.

College freed Dorothy, but it was the women's movement that transformed her. At twenty-three, she was still living in Florida, taking graduate courses in anthropology, editing a feminist magazine, and volunteering at a child-care center. She was exhausted from overwork, despairing of the pain in her past, and "near suicidal" over a failing love affair when she attended her first consciousness–raising group at a Tallahassee women's center. And there, everything changed.

"There was a woman sitting across from me in a beanbag chair. She was wearing pearls—I can still remember those pearls," says Dorothy. "The woman began to talk quietly about a dream that she was having, a dream of loading up a shotgun, driving through the night, and killing the father who had abused her."

In *Skin: Talking About Sex, Class and Literature*, Dorothy writes movingly about how those words affected her. "She was as close to breaking as I felt myself, as desperate and alone. I wanted to touch her, not like a lover but like family, to offer comfort and love and hope. Instead I offered her the one unfailing gift of my family—bitter humor. I gave a little laugh and told her 'I'll do yours if you do mine.' It was the first time I had told anyone I wanted to kill my stepfather."

Dorothy began to speak more openly about her history of violence, and to write with a new focus and fervor. She had been writing since she was in her early teens, but each year she burned everything she wrote in a ritual bonfire, annihilating her poems, in-progress novels, and journals full of thoughts and ideas. Now, encouraged by the women who had become her alternative family, she began to keep her writing, ignoring the "terrible drive" to destroy her work. In saving her writing, she began to save herself.

Over the course of the next decade, Dorothy moved steadily northward ("one woman at a time"), finally settling in Brooklyn to take classes in anthropology at the New School for Social Research. And she wrote, publishing her first book of poetry in 1983 and a short story collection in 1988.

Those books were informed by Dorothy's decision to reconnect with the women in her family in the early eighties. She returned to Greenville out of a desire for reconciliation, a need for greater understanding, and a growing sense that to leave behind your history is to leave behind pieces of yourself.

That reconciliation was made possible by what she calls an "exacting," but largely unspoken, agreement with her mother, who was still married to Dorothy's stepfather. Dorothy would visit infrequently and never talk about why she did not come home more often. She must not confront her stepfather or indulge in any public expression of anger toward him. Even when calling home, she was discouraged from being "cold" if he answered the phone. She might feel rage, but she must never, ever express it.

Dorothy accepted all of this out of a desire to remain connected to her mother. It was never easy: even the most casual interaction with her stepfather might cause Dorothy to vomit—"my body just would not let me go on pretending nothing was wrong"—so visits home were most often cut short. Dorothy says that one of her greatest regrets is that this robbed her of her last chances to see her mother, who by then was struggling with the cancer that killed her at the age of fifty-six, just months before Dorothy turned in her manuscript for *Bastard Out of Carolina*.

Regret, and not rage, seems to characterize Dorothy's feelings about being asked to choose between spending time with her mother or staying away from the man who had abused her. I have no doubt that the rage is there—Dorothy has said that in her twenties, she was so angry with her mother that she could not even speak to her by phone, and much of her early work explores the theme of maternal failure with blistering candor. Still, those literary expressions of anger feel small when set against her devotion to her mother.

The great mystery of Dorothy's life—at least when viewed from the outside—may be her relationship to Ruth Ann Gibson. I use the present tense because in a very real way, and clearly by design, Dorothy has kept her mother's memory alive since her passing in 1990. *Bastard Out of Carolina* is dedicated to her, a dedication that I thought must have been pointed until I met Dorothy and listened to her speak about her mother with both honesty and deep affection. In the years since her mother's death, Dorothy has published essays, a memoir, and a particularly touching homage in *O, The Oprah Magazine* that explore, often candidly and always lovingly, Ruth Ann's life, influence, and choices. She has said that she is "writing to save the dead," and especially to save her mother.

I was unprepared for the depth and intensity of Dorothy's devotion to her mother when we met. In fact, knowing the general outline of their history from *Bastard Out of Carolina*, I came to my first meeting with Dorothy outraged with her mother on her behalf. But talk to Dorothy at any length, and the Ruth Ann she describes comes alive in such a way that you begin to believe in the "unquestioning, absolute, and painful" love that she and Dorothy had for one another. The mother Dorothy describes was physically affectionate, never too weary to be witty—"Mama gifted me with my humor and these good teeth"—and possessed of a serious work ethic and a quiet dignity.

Ruth Ann was painfully aware of the way that her family was viewed by the broader community, so she taught her daughters to demand respect. "Never back down. Never drop your eyes. People look at you like a dog, you dog them." That she imparted these lessons to Dorothy and her sisters is both poignant and perplexing in light of their mother's inability to insist that her daughters be treated this way at home.

Dorothy sees all of this, of course. She has said that she wrote *Bastard* in order to come to terms with the ways that the mother who loved her so tenderly could fail her so spectacularly. Yet despite—or because of—their shared history, Dorothy loves her mother with ferocity and a tenderness that I have rarely encountered. No part of that love seems to be a product of denial. I suspect that there is nothing that we think we know about Dorothy Allison's relationship to her mother that she has not already considered herself.

Perhaps one of the reasons that Dorothy can grant her mother absolution is that Ruth Ann Gibson was also a victim of her husband's cruelty. Or perhaps the compassion with which Dorothy views her mother's life is the product of her brutally honest examination of her own complicity. "I come at my mother's life from my own; I remember that I loved my little sisters but wanted them to sleep closest to the door," she has written.

For readers of *Bastard Out of Carolina*, the book's most heartbreaking passage is inevitably its ending, when Anney Boatwright, the character based on Dorothy's mother, discovers her daughter being raped, fights off the stepfather with the rage and contempt one might expect, and then, in response to his pleas and tears, agrees to stay with him, leaving Bone with an aunt. "God, I hated her mother in that moment," a friend who says that the book "changed her life" told me recently.

Dorothy views things differently. She says that she wrote the ending of *Bastard Out of Carolina* as an ideal, not a betrayal. "When you become a writer you begin to see the stories you've told yourself, the stories other people tell themselves. Then you start crafting it. What if? What if she'd left? *Bastard* is me telling myself the story of what would have happened if my mother had had the good sense to leave me."

Near the end of her life, as Ruth Ann was dying of cancer, she expressed her grief and guilt to Dorothy. "I should have left him,"

Dorothy remembers her saying. "But each time I thought I would, something happened."

The apology, Dorothy says firmly, was not necessary. "Mama did what she felt she had to do and did it from a place of love. I was angry in my twenties and hurting in my thirties, but by the time she died, I was past all that. I felt only love, not rage. And I wanted to make sense of her story, which is what *Bastard* is all about."

The rage Dorothy feels toward her stepfather seems, at first blush, less nuanced. "I chose to let the son of a bitch live," she has said, and the comment is pure Dorothy: part bravado, part bluster, and all good story. The truth is more complex. For years, she returned home and avoided confrontation, silencing herself to be able to see her mother. And though her loathing of her stepfather is palpable—it manages to feel both hot and cool, all at once—she has also spoken eloquently about how the contempt and violence the world too often visits on poor and marginalized men can be internalized and then acted out within their homes.

For Dorothy, a fundamental question is how we view children—something she has thought a lot about since becoming a parent herself. In *Conversations with Dorothy Allison*, a collection of interviews with the author, Dorothy notes that her mother's immediate and extended family were loving and fiercely loyal but somehow didn't "believe in" children. "They thought children were really powerful, strong adults masquerading in children's bodies, which is a vicious thing to believe . . . especially when you believe it about yourself."

All of this seems worlds away from the life Dorothy has built for herself today. She is an in-demand lecturer and visiting writing instructor, traveling often to mentor the aspiring young authors she affectionately refers to as her "baby writers." Attend one of her book readings, and you'll find a gorgeous melting pot of book lovers, literary critics, gay and lesbian activists, sexual violence survivors, Southern expatriates, and "the occasional guy in a Peterbilt hat" who may have discovered her writing when *Bastard* was carried at Costco (a retail placement dear to Dorothy's working-class heart).

Having overcome, all those years ago, the desire to destroy her own writing, the home Dorothy shares with Alex and Wolf Michael is lined with bookshelves full of journals and file cabinets bursting with works-in-progress. She writes ceaselessly, filling notebooks with snatches of overheard conversation, song lyrics—Steve Earle and Lucinda Williams were in heavy rotation when I interviewed her— and suddenly recalled pieces of accidental brilliance one of her aunts may have said. The "may" is critical, because Dorothy's memories are always steeped in her own vibrant imagination.

After years of guilt, recrimination, and blame, she is close to her sisters—"we are all mothers, and having that in common has helped"—and as loyal to her extended family as she is honest about them. Most of them still live in the South. Do they read her books? "Honey, I am lucky," she laughs. "I don't hail from a family of readers. They buy my books, and it's a big family, so that is no small thing. Then they keep 'em on the shelf and wait until the movie comes out" (*Bastard* and Dorothy's 1998 best-selling novel, *Cavedweller*, were both made into films).

Dorothy still struggles with the guilt that characterizes those who escape their impoverished beginnings. "You leave people behind— that's part of the deal. For every one of us who makes it out, there are dozens more who will never even get the chance. It's one of the reasons I write: to make the world a little less mean, to get people inside of another human being long enough for them to start to care about that person."

Does she think of the past often? By way of an answer, she tells me about a recent conversation she had with her sister, who attended a funeral service for a family friend buried in the same cemetery where Ruth Ann Gibson was laid to rest years ago. After the other mourners went home, Dorothy's sister stayed behind, pulling together a bouquet of flowers from the abundance of blossoms left at the fresh gravesite—"My sister didn't want those blooms to go to waste," Dorothy says, "and she surely thought those flowers wouldn't be much missed by the newly departed, bless her soul"—and took them to their mother's gravesite. There she discovered that their stepfather— who had outlived Ruth Ann by a decade and a half—had been buried next to their mother.

Dorothy pauses at this point, and I see the flicker of a struggle in her eyes. Does she tell the story with dark humor, or acknowledge it as heartbreak? How do you craft a new ending when an ending that is so unjust—so unthinkable, really—has been set in stone? The silence between us lasts just a beat longer than her previous pauses. It is the silence of a woman, never at a loss for words, deciding that this time, she is not going to speak.

My America

I grew up in the sort of Midwestern small town regularly referred to as "The Real America," a description that seems to all but guarantee that the region being so labeled will in no way resemble most of the nation.

Wheaton, Illinois, is largely white, reliably conservative, and almost exclusively Christian, with more churches per capita than any other city in the nation (if the Genus Edition of Trivial Pursuit is to be believed). With its sweeping lawns, un-ironic picket fences, and state championship football teams, it's a town that spawned both *Saturday Night Live* legend John Belushi and Watergate investigative journalist Bob Woodward. This makes perfect sense to those of us who grew up there: a profane sense of humor, and an appreciation for the fact that things are not always as they seem, can serve you well in Wheaton.

My parents considered themselves progressives—it sometimes felt like they were the only liberals in the entire town. But my mother was a beloved grade-school teacher who was disinclined to discuss politics or religion with any vehemence. And my siblings and I had been raised to be high-achieving, non-confrontational, and polite in the extreme—a trifecta of qualities that seemed to cancel out our deviations from Wheaton's political norms, such as the occasional school paper editorial arguing for the rights of striking workers, or the loud-enough-for-the-neighbors-to-hear playing of the Rolling Stones' "Sympathy for the Devil" on Sundays. Even my father, a cigarette-smoking, Henry David Thoreau–reading environmentalist—we like our contradictions in my family—was largely tolerated in Wheaton (mostly because he was married to my mother).

The truth is that though I wanted desperately to get out of Wheaton, and decried my hometown in the way that any self-respecting teenager with liberal pretensions should, I wasn't entirely unhappy there. It was a place that represented the myth of America, and growing up there, I was almost never touched by our country's colder, harder facts. Over the dinner table, my father might heap scorn on businessmen (in his vernacular, "businessman" meant anyone who was not a teacher or a doctor) and rage against Ronald Reagan's gutting of the Environmental Protection Agency. But those businessmen were our neighbors, and the sky was clear and blue over Wheaton, Illinois. My father was raging against a machine that remained an abstraction to his own children—in fact, it was a machine that had largely benefitted us. It took a long time for the implications of that contradiction to make any sort of sense to me.

When I left home—first for college, then to work for a Washington, DC-based grassroots lobbying and communications agency focused on a list of social issues that included the AIDS crisis—I was afforded a very different view of America. But it was the experience of being kidnapped and raped at the age of twenty-five that created the clearest through-line between my innocence and knowing.

The American criminal justice system had failed badly in my case: the man who raped me was a convicted felon who had been granted leave from DC's Lorton Prison as part of a controversial work release program. Yet that same criminal justice system pursued, caught, and successfully prosecuted the man who attacked me, putting him away for life. The US attorney, the DC beat cops and detectives, and the FBI agents assigned to my case were, without exception, kind and respectful during what became an eighteen-month judicial process. But the transactional nature of our relationship was never lost on me:

they were driven by a cool, unquestioning pragmatism. This was a winnable case, and I was a credible (read: educated, articulate, white, seemingly blameless) crime victim. In the American legal system, where neat narratives win the day, this mattered. And that meant that I mattered, too.

Also not lost on me was the fact that my experience, to the degree that it was positive, was not the norm for those coming forward with charges of rape. I was vaguely aware of this as my case played out in the DC legal system. During the long months after my assault, I spent a lot of time waiting, always waiting, outside of the grand jury hearing rooms and attorneys' offices and police stations. And while I waited, I watched. I would have had to have been a fool, or willfully obtuse, not to see that other DC crime victims—largely black, most often poor, and sometimes drug-addicted or prostituted—were not always treated with the same courtesy that I was afforded.

At the time, I felt only vaguely conflicted about this. I was too wrapped up in my own grief and shock to take on anyone else's. But over time, and as I began interviewing survivors of sexual violence for the documentary project that became this book, my vague discomfort over the largely favorable treatment I had received evolved into a full-fledged sense of guilt. It's not that I felt I deserved less. It's that so many other rape victims deserve more.

"It is different," Charlotte Pierce-Baker, the author of *Surviving the Silence: Black Women's Stories of Rape*, a collection of survivor testimonies that explore the intersection of race and rape, said to me recently. Then, Charlotte, a close friend who is ever thoughtful and cautious, amends her statement slightly: "It's more accurate to say that it *often* is different. America is not a colorblind society, or a classless society, and that affects rape victims. Still."

Politicians and pundits and PBS documentarians talk about the "American experience," but in truth there is no such thing. There are instead American experiences—millions of them—and the collective story that they tell can be as brutal as it is beautiful.

I found myself thinking quite a lot about all of this when I traveled in 2013 to the West African nation of Senegal. I was the only American member of a large delegation of artists and activists brought together by Art Works for Change, an organization that uses arts programs to raise awareness of human rights, social justice, and environmental issues. We had come to engage Senegalese students in a dialogue about gender-based violence, an ambitious but critically important task in a country where an upsurge in group rapes and the persistence of female genital cutting (FGC) are both pressing issues. And from the moment that I touched down in Dakar, Senegal's capital, my American identity was a focal point.

"Are you an American?" was invariably one of the first questions I was asked when meeting people, and my "Yes, I'm from Chicago," was always met with a fresh round of effusions, often expressed in English: *I love America! President Obama! Kanye! Can I listen to your iPod?* It was America-love as a series of T-shirt slogans, genuine but light as air. And almost everywhere I went, I encountered some version of it.

Yet toward the end of our trip, in the Kolda region of Senegal, I encountered a view of America that was moving in a different and far deeper way. A group of female elders—referred to by the Senegalese as *les grand-mères*—had joined our delegation at a local middle school in order to reinforce our antiviolence message. On the makeshift dais that morning, I was seated next to Kun Kande Balde, a Senegalese woman of about seventy. Kun Kande was soft spoken and elegant, dressed in a blue and gold boubou, the voluminous traditional gown with matching head wrap that more traditional Senegalese women often favor. She spoke Fula and French, and I spoke English (and barely any French), so we talked as best we could before she rose to address the hundreds of students assembled under an ancient baobab tree in the sand and dirt schoolyard.

And then this dignified, quiet woman began to speak, and she became a new person altogether. To say that Kun Kande spoke is actually an understatement: what she did was command. She had a powerful, ringing voice, and as she addressed the students in French, she gestured and reached upward and then outward with both hands, rocking and swaying to her own words. The United Nations representative seated next to me interpreted so that I could understand what she was saying.

Kun Kande shared the story of her own history of violence and spoke of the violence visited upon millions of African women before

Kun Kande Balde (left) with Anne Ream

her. She told the students that forced marriage and female genital cutting were—at last—against Senegalese national law, gesturing triumphantly with her right fist as she said those words. And she called on the girls present to use their own voices in the fight to end violence. "You must express yourselves! You must not be quiet about what is happening to you, to your daughters, to your mothers!"

She then turned, gestured to me, and cried out, "Your stories matter so much that even the Americans have come to hear you!" In response to this, the students applauded and stamped their feet in the dirt school courtyard, as a "*Les English sont ici!*" floated into the air with the billowing dust.

I was actually the only American present, but no matter. I was a symbol of something bigger and broader, a stand-in for a country that loomed so large here that an African elder who had never set foot on its shores invoked it to add force to her call for an end to gender-based violence. Her America was not primarily a place, or an idea, or even an ideal. It was a promise.

America, of course, has always been very good at promise. But our actual progress on women's issues has far too often been of the two steps forward, one step back variety. I had left for Senegal during a silly, sad season in our national political life, the spring of 2013. Re-authorization of the Violence Against Women Act, the landmark civil law rights law passed in 1994 with bipartisan support, had been held up for months by extremists in Congress claiming that its vital programs were "feminist pork" (it ultimately passed). Fresh reports of sexual violence in the US military seemed to emerge almost daily. And despite the twenty-five-year struggle of women's rights and human rights advocates, the United States remains one of the few countries unwilling to ratify the United Nation's Convention on the Elimination of All Forms of Discrimination Against Women, a vital treaty designed to bring equality to women across the globe.

The chasm between our American laws and purported values on violence against women and the lived reality for millions of victims of such violence felt awfully wide to me when I left for West Africa. Yet here, America still serves as a beacon for women's rights.

In the now famous words of President Kennedy, a man who was himself no stranger to contradictions, Americans are "unwilling to witness or permit that slow undoing of those human rights to which this nation has always been committed, and to which we are committed today at home, and around the world." The dual obligation he summoned—creating a just nation and fighting for justice beyond our borders—is one we have not, as a nation, always met. But on much of the African continent, it is an obligation that is seen as essentially and truly American.

I did not think of any of this as Kun Kande walked back to her seat. What I thought about was the extraordinary power of her person, and her words. *Vous etes magnifique*, I wrote on a page I tore from my journal and handed to her as the next speaker rose to address the students. She read the note, turned, and pointed to me. "*Non, vous etes magnifique*," she said with a laugh. I was not sure if she meant me, or my country. Perhaps the distinction didn't much matter.

In the world according to the sentimentalists, this would be the moment when I see America through the eyes of someone who had never known its freedoms and come to love my country more deeply than I ever had before. But the feeling Kun Kande's words sparked in me was not love of country, but a sort of longing: I wanted America to more often be all of the glorious things it is believed to be. I wanted the promise of my country fulfilled.

I left Dakar a week later, flew through Paris, and was shocked back into my first-world sensibility by the luxury mall that is the Charles de Gaulle Airport. Twenty-four hours later, I was home. On the day I arrived, the *Chicago Tribune* reported that a Congo army battalion that stood accused of mass rape had been trained by the United States. Somewhere in a village in Senegal, a deep belief in the promise of America remained, undiminished. But here in the United States, it was time to get back to work.

The More Things Change:
Beth Adubato

The 112,000 signatures on the 2013 Change.org petition delivered to Secretary of Education Arne Duncan—a petition demanding that the federal government hold universities accountable for failing to protect students from sexual assault—were more than just names. They were a bundle of outrages, some of them decades old.

The women and men who signed it were calling for American universities to do things so basic, and so seemingly obvious, that the real shock was that a demand for action was needed at all: *Take rape charges seriously. Investigate them swiftly. Stop asking women who have been raped by a fellow student to "take a semester off." Start recognizing that when a popular young man commits sexual assault on campus, it is not a misunderstanding, a youthful indiscretion, or an infraction. It is a crime.*

The signers included college students who had been raped by a classmate and then denied justice by school administrators, university alumnae who had experienced similar violence and institutional failure decades earlier, professors grown tired of seeing their schools fail rape victims, and parents who had experienced the heartbreak of sending a child to college and seeing her come home a crime victim.

People signed the petition to the Department of Education in anger and sadness. But mostly, they signed the petition with stories: *This happened to my roommate. This happened to my daughter. This happened to me, last month. Last year. Too many years ago to even remember.*

Beth Adubato, an assistant professor at New York Institute of Technology, owned one of those stories. She was nineteen years old when she was raped while a student at The College of William and Mary, in Williamsburg, Virginia.

Attending William and Mary had been Beth's dream since she was a girl. She was a straight A student, and school was everything for her. "I was born on the same day as Thomas Jefferson—one of the earliest graduates of William and Mary—so for my college application, I wrote a really feminist essay about how I was going to be like him, someone who changed the world," Beth recalls.

She remembers the day she arrived at William and Mary, during the 1980s, as one of the happiest of her life. "Everything was new," Beth says. "Everything was beginning."

Beth became an active and engaged student. "I worked on campus, I lived on campus, I loved the William and Mary life." She was nineteen years old when a fellow student raped her. He was a popular lacrosse player Beth had met at a Friday night fraternity party. They spoke briefly, and when he offered to walk her home at the end of the evening, she remembers politely saying no. "I thought he was cute and nice, we all did," says Beth. "Maybe it was my sixth sense, but I told him good night and left with a girlfriend."

Later that night, he entered through the dorm-room door that Beth had left unlocked for her roommate and raped her repeatedly. A day later, it was discovered that someone had broken the building's exterior card-key lock.

The details of that night remain clear to Beth. She wishes that they didn't, but knows that there are some things she will never be able to forget. Yet Beth's memories of the days that followed are what most unsettle her.

"The rape was bad, but being blamed and denied any sort of justice was also horrible," Beth says. "It's that 'wrong on top of a wrong' that gets to you."

Two days after she was raped, Beth gave a statement to the William and Mary campus police. The officers suggested that she might be "crying rape"—she later learned that was what her assailant was saying happened—and asked Beth why she didn't fight back or scream. "It was a Friday night, the dorm was mostly empty, and he was a 265-pound athlete," Beth says. "To me, it made perfect sense that I didn't scream. But not to them." The campus police also suggested that the rug burns on Beth's back could have been the result of "bad sex."

During her examination at the campus health center on the Monday following the rape, Beth recalls that the doctor was "perfectly nice and promptly told me that my transferring from William and Mary would be for the best," Beth recalls. If she stayed, the school could offer her counseling at the hands of a graduate student in the psychology department.

Beth didn't transfer—physically—but she says that, in a very real sense, she ceased to be a student at William and Mary after she was raped. The university's decision to abandon its investigation of the lacrosse player who had raped her—a determination made by the then-dean of students—was devastating for Beth. She was confident that evidence and student witnesses could have corroborated her testimony that she had not chosen to go home with the student who raped her, but William and Mary was intent on "moving forward."

Beth wishes she could have done the same. Instead, she was ostracized by William and Mary students who had previously been her friends and treated like a troublemaker by people who didn't know her at all. A handful of lacrosse players followed her when they saw her between classes, a way of intimidating Beth without technically doing anything wrong.

Beth began to avoid people and parties—"anyone Greek, anyone athletic, anyone 'popular'"—and felt sick with anxiety when she went to her classes. "You know when you are a pariah, and I was," says Beth. "You feel it emotionally, and you feel it physically. I was literally sick to my stomach from nerves."

It did not take long in this environment for Beth's personality to change. "I was so depressed that I stopped caring about school," Beth says. "My post-rape self did not resemble my pre-rape self, or my high school self, at all. I withdrew completely."

One of the hardest lessons Beth learned during that time was about the limitations of loyalty. After she was raped, several of her closest female friends distanced themselves from Beth but continued to speak to the lacrosse player who had assaulted her. Beth had been a good student and had what she believed were solid relationships with her professors. Yet they, too, made it clear that they didn't want to hear Beth's story.

"People will do anything to pretend someone they think they know wouldn't commit rape," Beth says. "He was a popular athlete at a school that loves its lacrosse players. Very few people—not the dean of students, not my friends, not the other students—wanted to admit that he was also a rapist."

So complete was the failure of those around Beth that the one example of someone defending her stands out in her memory, even now: "My friend Lee almost punched a guy in his fraternity, someone who was talking me down, even though that guy was a foot taller than he was," says Beth. "It was the only time someone stuck up for me."

The following year, Beth moved off the William and Mary campus. "I tried to create a whole new life for myself—working off campus, taking dance classes, immersing myself in theater. And I made a new set of friends," Beth says. "It was coping in one way, but it also interfered with my academics. I couldn't go to school and be terrified at school. You just can't do both."

Two semesters short of graduating, Beth left William and Mary and returned to Montclair, New Jersey, her hometown. She does not see the decision to leave as much of a decision at all. She was struggling emotionally, academically, and physically at William and Mary. "I could not stay another day. I'm pretty amazed," she says, "that I stayed as long as I did."

Unaware of why the daughter and granddaughter who had once excelled had become "such a failure-dropout," Beth's family was limited in its sympathy. "I blame myself for that, because I needed to ask for their help, to tell them that I had been raped," Beth says. "But I was so ashamed and depressed that I just didn't have the words."

Beth's sympathy for herself was limited as well. "I probably needed to get myself in therapy or to a good rape crisis center, confront what had happened." Beth says. "But instead I drifted for a long, long time. People would say, 'Oh, where did you go to college?' or 'Beth, didn't you go to William and Mary?' How do you say, 'Yes, college was great. And then I was raped'?"

It took Beth more than a decade to re-enroll in school. In the interim, she worked a series of lower-paying jobs, got married, and had her daughter, Allegra, "the single most amazing gift to come during that time." But the idea of being back on a college campus remained daunting.

"That really says something about what rape does to you," Beth says, "because my whole identity, my whole life, had been about excelling at school. And I was not ready to go back." But time was healing, and the gravitational pull of earning her degree proved powerful. So in the nineties, Beth applied to Rutgers University, a school close to her home and the life she had built for her daughter. She had been accepted at Rutgers years earlier, when she decided to instead attend William and Mary, so it felt right to her. "I was hopeful again," Beth says. "I had my daughter now, and I wanted to be a good role model for her. And I knew that I had a lot to offer."

During the application process, Beth was contacted by Lydia Rodriguez, a Rutgers dean who was reviewing her application. Dean Rodriguez was perplexed by Beth's grades from the semester in which she had left William and Mary.

"I had asked for a medical withdrawal from William and Mary during that last semester, but the administration never bothered to tell my professors," says Beth. "Unbeknownst to me, there were five F's on my school record. When Dean Rodriguez saw that I had gone from being an A student to failures across the board, she knew that something must have gone wrong. And she had the decency to reach out to me about it.

"I told her the whole story, about being raped, about what had happened after, about why I left school," Beth says. She remembers Lydia Rodriguez growing very quiet over the phone and then saying, "Beth, you should never have to tell that story unless you want to tell it. Those grades should have been expunged with your medical withdrawal."

A few days later, Beth received a second call—she believes it was probably prompted by Lydia Rodriguez—from the dean at William and Mary who had, years earlier, declined to pursue the investigation into the lacrosse player who had raped her. He had since been promoted and taken on an even larger administrative role at the school. Somewhat to Beth's surprise, her former dean apologized to Beth for what had happened years earlier. And then he told her that he had gained a "better understanding" of what she'd gone through after his own daughter was raped.

Beth's feelings about that call are nuanced. "Hearing his voice on the phone brought me back to that horrible meeting all those years back, when he said, 'William and Mary is not taking this case further,'" says Beth. "And it was practically re-traumatizing to hear from him again.

"On a human level, I know that he was trying to connect, to tell me that he finally 'got rape' because it had come close to home," Beth continues. "But you shouldn't just care when it happens to your daughter. You should care when it happens to any of us."

Beth says that receiving her undergraduate degree from Rutgers in 1996—she went on to receive her PhD in criminal justice from the school a few years later—was "quite possibly the best day of my life. Rape took all of those years from me," Beth says. "But I looked out at my daughter during my graduation—she was five years old at the time—and just thought, 'Yes. We've got our lives back.'"

While she was an undergraduate at Rutgers, Beth began to speak out about having been raped years earlier. She was taking a criminology class when a much younger student expressed the opinion that so-called acquaintance rape was something that women usually made up. Beth remembers feeling so compelled to speak that her story practically told itself. "I was furious—I *had* to speak up," Beth says, "because those beliefs cost college women their lives."

The classroom conversation that followed her disclosure that day was made possible at least in part by an "amazing" Rutgers University criminology professor, Todd Clear. "He wanted the students to think about rape in a 'real-world' way, and there I was with my real-world story," says Beth. "He encouraged me and supported me after I spoke. But he also made sure that the other students knew that my story was not an uncommon one—it represented a real criminal justice problem."

Beth is convinced that talking about her rape outside of the classroom is just as vital. "My daughter and her friends, they all know that I was raped during college, by the cute, popular guy everyone admired," Beth says.

"I'm a mom, so of course I want to teach them to be careful," Beth says. "But I also want to teach them to support other girls and women, to never pre-judge, because no one claims to be raped on a lark."

A new generation of college activists understands this all too well. The drivers of the Change.org petition delivered to Secretary Duncan in the summer of 2013 call themselves Know Your IX. A loose collective of hundreds of rape survivors and their allies from over fifty universities, Know Your IX is using federal law and the media to force administrators to respond to reports of campus rape. Named for Title IX of the Education Amendments of 1972, which requires that colleges that receive federal funding investigate and resolve campus rape and sexual assault charges or lose federal resources, Know Your IX is facilitating change on a national level.

Individually, Know Your IX members are speaking out about being raped and denied justice—at Yale, Amherst, University of Southern California, and dozens of schools in between—and filing a series of lawsuits that put teeth in such claims. Collectively, they have become a national anti-rape force. By the end of July 2013, the Department of Education's Office of Civil Rights had received forty-eight complaints regarding Title IX violations related to campus rape and sexual abuse, more complaints than it had received in any full previous year.

Members of the Know Your IX collective say that their present-day successes are informed by past stories like Beth's. "These stories are not new," says Dana Bolger, an Amherst senior and Know Your IX cofounder who helped create the Change.org petition. "When you realize that you are part of a long line of college women who have stories like yours, going back into the seventies, eighties, nineties— you know you have to act," says Dana.

Rates of rape and sexual assault have been largely constant over the last forty years: every credible study points to the fact that between one-quarter to one-fifth of college women will experience rape or attempted rape before graduating.

"These violations have occurred because the consequences for universities failing to do the right things were not seen as steep enough," says Stacy Malone, the executive director of the Victim Rights Law Center in Boston, the first nonprofit law center in the nation solely dedicated to serving the legal needs of sexual assault victims.

"A new generation of survivors is using the web to connect and information-share, to make legal demands in coordinated ways," says Stacy. "When they use social media to say, 'This happened to me at my school, and here's what I did to fight back,' it's really powerful."

Beth Adubato loves seeing all of that power. A professor at the New York Institute of Technology, she says the best part of her job is spending her days with students who make her feel "hopeful about the future." But when she learned about the Change.org petition to Secretary Duncan, she felt a unique sort of awe and gratitude.

"I knew that what William and Mary was doing was wrong," Beth says. "But it took me years to understand that what they did was actually illegal. I didn't know enough about my rights to even grasp that they had been violated. I don't think I'd even heard of Title IX. Seeing over one hundred thousand people signing on and saying, 'This is not OK?' That's a fantastic feeling."

But the thrill Beth feels about the progress being made is tempered by a single, painful fact: sexual violence on college campuses still occurs at an alarming rate. Beth knows that the right university response to a student who has been raped can be "life changing." She just wishes that such a response wasn't necessary in the first place.

"You dream of a world without rape," Beth says. "But it's hard, some days, to believe that it will ever happen."

Defiance: **Tory Bowen Flynn**

There is a startling, almost Technicolor quality to Tory Bowen. "She reminds me of Brenda Starr," I scribble in my notes after our first meeting, and later, as I ponder that description, I conclude that it is neither Tory's red hair, nor the comic-strip perfection of her features that leaves me with this impression. It's something about her affect. She is vivid—sometimes even dramatic—in her manner and speech, but seriousness seems to underscore each word and gesture. As she walks toward me in the crowded coffee shop in Washington, DC, where we first meet, I know that her heels are clicking even before I hear them. This is a woman in a focused, purposeful hurry.

Tory was Los Angeles born and bred, the child of two successful seventies-era television actors, and perhaps this explains something of her bearing. Uninterested in a life in Hollywood, she decamped for the Midwest not long after graduating from high school. It's a sort of reverse exodus that says something about her willingness to surprise and defy. "I was never a typical 'California girl,' and acting was not where I wanted to be. What interested me was leadership and government. When I went to the University of Nebraska, I think some of my LA friends thought it was crazy."

While attending Nebraska, Tory became active in her campus sorority and landed a coveted internship in then–US senator Chuck Hagel's office. "I really felt like I had made the right choice in coming to the Midwest," says Tory. "So much good was happening for me there."

Tory remembers little about the night that she was raped. "It was Halloween 2004, and I was a senior in college. I had gone out with a group of my sorority sisters to a local college bar. I had a few drinks and at one point had a drink where I remember nothing after. Everything just went black."

Tory woke up seven hours later, naked, with vomit encrusted in her hair and an unknown man on top of her. "As soon as I came to, I screamed 'No, get off of me,' and he stopped raping me. But I had no idea what had happened to me during those hours when I was in a coma state and no idea how he got me there. I felt sick, violated, angry, and every other emotion in between." Without her cell phone, shoes, or keys, Tory had to ask this unknown man—who refused to tell her his name and would only share his initials—to drive her home. "It was humiliating and scary to be vulnerable like that," says Tory. "When I got home, I was crying hysterically when my roommate answered the door—without my keys, I had to knock—and the first words I said to her were 'I've been taken advantage of.' I guess I was not yet ready to say the word 'rape.'"

Tory's roommate took her to the hospital and Tory reported the crime to the police. Pamir Safi was identified and arrested twenty days later, thanks to Tory's police report and other witnesses from that night. Tory learned later that Safi had been arrested for rape before. "I felt sickened and sad, knowing that other women had gone through this," says Tory. "But it also strengthened my resolve to testify against him. I thought that any jury in the world would see that I had been raped."

In 2006, the case came to trial in Lincoln, Nebraska, with Lancaster County Court Judge Jeffre Cheuvront presiding. Trials often take surprising turns, but neither Tory nor the state's attorney prosecuting her case anticipated what would happen next. Clarence Mock, the defense attorney for Safi, successfully argued that Tory should be restricted from using the words *rape*, *sexual assault*, *victim*, and *assailant* during her trial testimony, pointing to a thirty-two-year-old law barring terms that pose the risk of "unfair prejudice, confusion of the issues, or misleading the jury."

"Trials should be deliberations based upon the facts and not about who can think up the most juicy terms to apply," Mock said in making his case. Of course, there is nothing "juicy" about the terms rape or sexual assault, which describe crimes of a heinous nature. Yet Judge

Cheuvront sided with the defense, instructing Tory to refrain from using those terms while on the stand. She was instructed to say "had sex" or "intercourse" instead. The ruling imposed the same language restrictions on the police, the prosecution, and the other witnesses—including two women who were set to testify that they had also been raped by Safi. The jury was not made aware of the ruling.

It was a turn of events that left Tory literally and figuratively speechless. "I had never 'had sex' with this man. Telling me to say that instead of allowing me to say that he had raped me was telling me to commit perjury. But the judge threatened me with jail time, fines, or a mistrial if I said the word rape. So I felt placed in an impossible situation."

When Tory took the stand to testify, she realized exactly how impossible it was. "I kept having to stop each time I wanted to say 'rape,' mentally correct myself, and then say 'had sex' instead. Those words did not describe what had been done to me, which was bad enough. But even worse was the fact that my pauses, my correcting myself each time I wanted to say rape but couldn't, that made me seem unsure to the jurors. And they had no idea why I was hesitating."

Given the language restrictions imposed on the witnesses, few were surprised when that first trial ended with a hung jury. It was an outcome that left Tory angry, but also transformed.

"During that original trial, I tried to be 'good,' abiding by the ruling," says Tory. "I tried to work within the system, hoping that despite the fact that I felt the judge was very wrong, the system would work for me. But it didn't. After that, I decided that I would not make the mistake of believing in the system again."

When a second trial was scheduled, and Tory learned that she would face the same language restrictions, she and her legal team fought back. While prosecutors and her own attorney challenged Judge Cheuvront's ruling in the court of law, Tory appealed to the court of public opinion. "I spoke out publicly because people needed to know what was being done in the name of justice. And I spoke out because I had come to believe that this was bigger than me. I never thought of this as 'my story.' It was a story I was telling for every woman who had ever been raped and then treated unfairly in the court of law."

Tory's desire to speak out was, by all indications, contagious. Anti-violence advocates soon learned about the case, and a national advocacy organization, PAVE (Promoting Awareness, Victim Empowerment), organized a series of protests in response to Judge Cheuvront's decision. When activists who opposed the ruling showed up outside the courthouse and at locations across the country with their mouths taped shut, holding posters with the words Tory was not allowed to say, the local and national media quickly took notice. "Suddenly, people were talking, not just about my case but about what this said about the barriers that rape victims can face in the legal system," says Tory.

All of this was more than Tory had expected but exactly the sort of attention she felt the case deserved. "If protests were going to be what it took to change things, I was totally OK with that. I understood that the press could send a message in a way I couldn't alone."

Tory was a realist who also remained an optimist. "I actually hoped that once Judge Cheuvront saw and heard that so many people—respected victims groups, advocacy organizations, attorneys, journalists—thought that these language restrictions were not right, he would change his mind." It didn't work that way. Cheuvront instead declared a mistrial, asserting that nationwide protests and media attention had made a fair trial impossible. Despite an appeals process that ultimately went all the way to the United States Supreme Court, the case has never been re-tried, but was dismissed "with prejudice."

I ask Tory if the public outrage over her case provided an alternative form of justice for her. "Justice? I could never call this justice," she says. "The man who did this to me was never held accountable. But seeing hundreds of people across the country stand with me meant the world to me. Having other survivors say, 'Thank you for standing for this,' that was so powerful."

It is a difficult thing—at times a devastating thing—to testify at the trial of one's assailant. Victims are asked to return imaginatively to what is often the most painful chapter of their lives, and to do this before a judge, a jury, and the man whose violence has forever altered them. In a culture that too often blames and disbelieves victims, testifying is not only an act of faith—it is also a statement of hope. But as every woman who has contemplated reporting a rape is well aware, the risk to reward ratio can seem, and often is, painfully high. Over forty years after the advent of the rape crisis movement, the rape shield laws that once protected victims from having their sexual histories explored (and exploited) are challenged so often, and so successfully, that they almost seem to be a thing of the past. Defense attorneys do double duty as publicists, using the 24/7 cable news networks to plant seeds of doubt in the court of public opinion, in hopes that a few vines of disbelief will make their way into the court of law. The Rape, Abuse, and Incest National Network (RAINN) estimates that only 40 percent of rape victims report to police. Yet women like Tory Bowen still come forward, believing that even when the world does not wish to hear their testimony, the legal system is bound to do so.

The word *rape* is difficult for a jury to hear. But the act of rape is infinitely more difficult for a victim to live through, which is why the legal and cultural language that exists to describe such violation is so important for victims. Saying these words in a court of law—"I was raped, he raped me, I am a rape victim"—is an act not only of courage but also of clarity.

"Accurate and truthful testimony is part of the bedrock of our entire judicial system. The victim's willingness to participate in that system hinges on their belief that, while under oath, they can testify fully to their experience," notes Susan Estrich, a law professor at the University of Southern California Law School.

"Why can't we just call it what it is? It's rape," says Scott Berkowitz, president and founder of RAINN. "By banning this key word in describing a sexual assault, we are not acknowledging the seriousness of the crime in the court room."

The sexual violence that Tory Bowen lived through has shaped her life's work. "At the time of the trial, I thought I would become an attorney. But I realized through all of this that the court of public opinion is a very powerful force," says Tory. "Sharing my story helped me understand how important media is to our society, so I turned that into my career. And I love it—I love knowing that communicating ideas and policies accurately can lead to change."

Tory believes that rebuilding your life in the wake of sexual violence means embracing the unknown. "When you are going through this, you have no idea what your future has in store for you. The man I was dating during the trial stood by my side and went to protests and rallies with me. He stood by me as I spoke out. He is now my husband, and we have a beautiful daughter."

"The bible I carried with me and read from during my trial, and a dear friend who helped me regain the faith I lost after all of this happened became my inspirations for starting a ministry for sexual violence survivors. It took years for my life to unfold and to see that what was intended to do me harm, God was able to transform into good," says Tory.

But embracing what she believes is God's plan does not mean accepting what has happened to her. "I have a beautiful life, and I am very grateful for the tapestry I've woven, despite being raped," says Tory. "But this rape was a crime. Being silenced by the judge was a travesty. And whatever good has come out of this is not going to stop me from saying that."

Rachel Durchslag (left) and Brenda Myers-Powell

The Sisterhood:
Brenda Myers-Powell

"One is not born, but rather becomes a woman," the French philosopher Simone de Beauvoir wrote in her 1949 classic, *The Second Sex*. Her book is a historical exploration of the ways female identity is shaped, a reminder that girls come into the world a blank slate, but don't stay that way for very long.

Brenda Myers-Powell, the founder of the Dreamcatcher Foundation, an organization fighting sex trafficking, has lived, painfully, what de Beauvoir explores in print. She grew up on Chicago's West Side, a latchkey kid raised by an alcoholic grandmother who told her, insistently and often, that she would never amount to much. Brenda was molested from the age of five by an uncle and abused by a handful of other men who moved in and out of her grandmother's apartment. Violence was woven into the fabric of her life almost from its start.

"When we were little kids, my girlfriend Gloria and I would sit on the fire escape of our apartment building, watching 'the fights,'" Brenda says. "You know, men beating up their wives, the police being called, the woman going to the hospital to get stitches, the whole thing."

"The next day it would be that same woman, making him breakfast, telling the neighbors he was her man, acting like she didn't have a black eye," Brenda says. "We just thought, 'that's the way it is for us.'"

Prostitution also made a sort of terrible sense to an adolescent Brenda. "My uncle had been taking off my panties for years," Brenda says. "And I would look out onto the street, and I would watch these women—from a distance they seemed so beautiful, so shiny—getting paid for what was being done to me anyway. And I wanted to have some of that shine."

On Good Friday in 1973, a few days shy of her fifteenth birthday, Brenda walked to the corner of Division and Clark streets in Chicago and caught the attention of her first john. She remembers everything about that night: the cruel glare of the neon Mark Twain Hotel sign, her green, polyester, two-piece outfit—"so bad that it would almost fly today"—and the wig that she thought made her look more sophisticated (but couldn't have made her look much older).

In retrospect, Brenda says that that first night was frightening, degrading, and anything but glamorous. But to an adolescent girl who had known sexual violence and neglect for most of her life, it felt like power. "My grandmother always told me that I was too stupid to take care of myself," Brenda says. "But I made over $300 that night."

Not long after her first experience with prostitution, Brenda was pistol-whipped and kidnapped by two pimps and taken to an unknown location and raped. She was then prostituted at a series of rest stops. "They called that a 'pimp arrest,'" Brenda says. "It was how they told me that they were in control. It was trafficking, I see that now. Then, it just felt bad."

Brenda says that there are times when she wishes that the twenty-four years that followed were a blur. They are not. Prostitution was, for her, inherently degrading. It was also dangerous. Beatings and gun violence were commonplace. She was stabbed. To numb herself to the pain of the past, and the violence of her present, she became addicted to crack cocaine.

Brenda had entered prostitution in large part to flee childhood sexual abuse but soon discovered that rape was commonplace in the sex trade. "I don't even know how to answer the question, 'Were you ever raped as a prostitute?'" Brenda says. "Because johns know you can't go to the police if they rape you, so some of them will hurt you really bad."

In 1997, when Brenda was thirty-nine years old, a john pushed her from his car. Brenda's clothes caught in the car door as he sped off, dragging her for several blocks. Her injuries were extensive: she almost lost an eye, and the scars from the accident remain visible.

"When I was lying in the hospital, I realized two things," Brenda says. "I was not ready to die. And if I didn't get out, I was going to die."

Brenda may well have been correct. A comprehensive 2004 mortality study, funded by the National Institutes of Health and conducted by the *American Journal of Epidemiology*, shows that workplace homicide rates for women working in prostitution are fifty-one times that of the next most dangerous occupation for women (which is working in a liquor store). The average age of death of the women studied was thirty-four years old. Brenda knew none of this at the time, of course. What she did know was that she wanted her life to change.

Not long after Brenda was released from the hospital, she made her way to Genesis House, a Chicago home for prostituted women that was founded by Edwina Gateley, a lay Catholic missionary. Deeply social justice-focused, Edwina had spent her life ministering to the poor, the homeless, and the prostituted. Genesis House was an extension of her belief that healing was possible in a safe, nonjudgmental, and female-focused environment.

Brenda had previously known about Genesis House, but she had no idea how life altering it would prove to be for her. It wasn't just the rehabilitation and counseling programs offered. It was also the force that is Edwina Gateley.

"Edwina is a compassionate woman, but a powerful woman—she doesn't take any mess," Brenda says. "I had learned a lot of wrong lessons over the years. But I finally had my mentor, someone who could show me what it meant to be a strong, powerful female."

The community Edwina and Genesis House connected Brenda to was diverse. There were the other prostituted women at the facility, a group Brenda calls her "beautiful sisters." There were Genesis House supporters from the northern suburbs of Chicago. "I'd see those volunteer ladies coming, and I'd say, 'Girl, you come on in here,' because I wanted to learn something no one had ever taught me: how to cross my legs, how to dress, how to act at a dinner party. I could just watch and learn."

And there were the Catholic nuns at the Siena Center in Racine, Wisconsin, who welcomed the women from Genesis House to their community for a three-day spiritual retreat. "Those are my other sisters," Brenda laughs. "You want to learn about female power? You spend a few days with the nuns."

Brenda spent the next year and a half at Genesis House, rebuilding her life and deepening her bonds with this interconnected community of women. She wanted to stay long enough to get strong, but not so long that she was afraid of being on her own.

"When, for the first time, you are being told that you are priceless and beautiful—not because of your body, but because of your spirit—it's hard to leave," says Brenda. "But you have to take that with you and spread all that positive around."

Clean and sober, Brenda landed her first post-rehab job providing in-home care for the elderly (she was so popular in the West Side homes she worked in that she was promptly promoted to supervisor). Brenda's next job was a higher-paying position as a bill collector. "I'd be on that phone, telling someone that they needed to do the right thing and pay their debt, and I would just think, 'Brenda, you have finally made it.'"

Brenda talks about her life during her first few years after leaving prostitution with pride and a deep, almost sensual, pleasure. She loved doing her job well, reveled in having a predictable daily schedule, and took long bubble baths. She adopted a cat who became her constant companion, a male she named Aretha Franklin ("Who says a boy cat can't be a diva?").

Brenda read self-help books voraciously, partly for their content, partly because just seeing them on her night table reminded her that she had a self worth helping. And for a long, long time she gave up men. "Abstinence," Brenda says with a smile, "can be a beautiful thing."

But something gnawed at Brenda—a sense that she was meant for more. The one constant in her life had been her personal power: even during her darkest moments, she knew she was a leader. Other people knew it, too.

"Once years earlier, when I was in bad shape and in another bad place getting high, a guy I didn't even know—he was just there getting high with us—looked over at me and said, 'You're the pied piper, aren't you? People follow your lead, but you don't use it for good.' And he was right."

Brenda had remained connected to Genesis House after she left, frequently volunteering and helping other women who came into the program. One day a staff member called Brenda to say that a community organizer from the Chicago Coalition for the Homeless was interested in finding someone who could talk, from a personal perspective, to the Illinois legislature about sexual exploitation. Brenda immediately signed on.

Testifying before an Illinois Senate subcommittee in 2001, as part of a larger effort to shift law enforcement's attention to sex traffickers and people who buy sex, gave Brenda her first taste of what she calls "real power."

"I spoke mostly from my heart that day—it was the first time I ever told my story, so I hadn't really figured out how to do it," Brenda recalls. "But a light went on when I was speaking to those senators because they were listening to me. I wasn't afraid at all. I just told them the truth. I had my shine, and it felt so good."

In the wake of that first Senate appearance, Brenda began to lay the foundation for a full-time career as an activist. She started speaking out about sex trafficking and prostitution to local community groups. She founded the Dreamcatcher Foundation, a nonprofit that works with Chicago youth who are at risk of entering the sex trade.

And in 2008 Brenda helped launch the Human Trafficking Response Team at the Cook County Sheriff's Office, partnering with law enforcement to help recently arrested trafficked or prostituted women gain access to counseling, social services, and temporary housing that can keep them out of the sex trade. It's a program that's been lauded as a national model, but to Brenda it's just common sense. "Most women don't want to be in prostitution," Brenda says. "Help them find options, and that can lead to a new life."

People often tell Brenda that they're inspired by the way she's been made stronger by adversity. She says she's flattered by that praise, but she's not sure that it's true. "No one really does it all on their own," Brenda says. "It takes a village to get us through. We need our sisters here."

Sisterhood is, for Brenda, a sacred concept. She believes that it's the secret to changing the world—and she knows that it's what changed her. "One thing Edwina taught me was to surround myself with strong, beautiful women," Brenda says. "Watch them. Learn from them. Find your sisters, and you're gonna find your power."

Brenda's "sister search" is what brought her to Rachel Durchslag, the founder of the Chicago Alliance Against Sexual Exploitation, an organization focused on ending the demand for prostituted and trafficked women. The two first interacted at a meeting at the Chicago Coalition for the Homeless almost a decade and a half ago, and they've been close friends ever since. "When I met Rachel, it was a feeling of 'We're going to make some things happen here,'" Brenda says. "But it was as much about her spirit as it was about our shared work. Rachel is my little sister. She is the positive that we women need in our lives. "

Rachel remembers feeling that same connection. "It's a heavy topic, sex trafficking," she says. "But Brenda inspires so much confidence. Standing in a room next to her and talking to a group of high school boys about sexual exploitation isn't easy. But you're fearless when you're next to Brenda. How can you not be?"

The outreach that Brenda and Rachel are doing has become increasingly important in cities across the United States. The American public largely understands sex trafficking as a global industry, one that is financed on the pain of women and girls. What we too often fail to see is that it is also a local one.

Like their international counterparts, US-based traffickers and pimps use force and coercion to recruit vulnerable young girls and boys into prostitution. Often homeless and victims of previous sexual or physical abuse, as Brenda was, they are then transported from cities, suburbs, and small-town communities to work in conditions that are degrading and dangerous. "We're not going to change this by punishing women who are already hurting," Brenda says. "It changes when we start looking at the johns who are buying sex and the pimps who are profiting from this big business."

The sex trade in the United States is a billion-dollar business. The vast majority of prostituted women and girls enter the sex trade while still in their teens. Over 80 percent are physically assaulted by their pimps and johns. The Federal Bureau of Investigation estimates that 293,000 American youth are currently at risk of becoming victims of commercial sexual exploitation.

Facts like this are often shocking to the public. But they make perfect sense to Brenda. "Getting caught up in the sex trade is easier than people know," she says. "Getting a woman out? That's the hard part."

Jenny Bush and her father, Steve Bush

In the Name of the Daughter: Steve and Jenny Bush

He is an unlikely political activist: a small businessman, a veteran, and the son of red state Republicans who believe deeply in the US military and don't much believe in questioning it. "I wasn't raised to challenge the system, not at all," Steve Bush says, reflecting on growing up in Goldwater-era Arizona. "Things changed for me after what happened to Jenny."

We were sitting at an outdoor café talking about fathers and daughters and what happens to a parent when the child he loves is raped. The child in this case is Steve's daughter, Jenny Bush. "You feel responsible—you are the man who was always supposed to protect your daughter, no matter how old she is. But there's no way to go back and stop it from happening. You just have to move forward," says Steve, looking at the crowds walking by, "because everything keeps going, doesn't it?"

To say that there is a sadness about Steve doesn't feel quite right—he is too focused, too intense, too obviously a man on a mission to seem sad. But he is often wistful when he talks about Jenny, and during especially painful points in my first conversation with him, he looks down, pauses, and his eyes fill. But within moments, he is again looking me in the eye, almost visibly shaking off the memory that took him elsewhere, because he has work to do. That work is the passage of Jenny's Law, which would bar veterans convicted of the most heinous sex crimes from being buried with honors in our national cemeteries.

Up until and even after James Allen Selby, a veteran of the Persian Gulf War, raped Jenny, it would have never occurred to the Bush family that such a bill would be necessary. They initially weren't focused on the fact that Selby was a veteran at all. They were focused on being there for Jenny, who was twenty-one at the time that Selby entered her home through a first-floor window, used duct tape to gag and bind her, and then raped her at knifepoint before fleeing.

After freeing herself, Jenny had the courage to report the crime to police and the conviction to pursue legal justice. Following a nationwide manhunt, Selby was apprehended and accused of raping thirteen women and girls, including Jenny, who took the stand at his trial. In October 2004, he was convicted on twenty-seven counts. Just hours before facing sentencing, Selby hanged himself in a Tucson jail.

For Selby's victims and their families, it may have been tempting to believe that in some larger sense the man had been held accountable. His suicide put a fine point on how little he had left to live for in the wake of his conviction. But his death also granted this serial rapist a moral reprieve that the civilian legal system didn't. Selby was a veteran and so, in accordance with Pentagon policy, he was buried with full military honors at Fort Sill National Cemetery in Oklahoma.

The military policy of allowing honors burials for veterans convicted of rape sends a chilling message to victims: even the most heinous sexual violence does not trump prior military service. It is a position that is as ethically indefensible as it is inconsistent. In 1997, after army veteran Timothy McVeigh was sentenced to death for his role in the Oklahoma City bombings, Congress barred veterans convicted of capital murder from being buried with full military honors. Today, veterans convicted of rape encounter no such restrictions, unless they have been sentenced to life in prison, a rarity in rape cases.

"I was shocked and upset. I think all of the victims were," says Jenny. "We had done the right thing and testified so that he would be punished for what he did, not buried like a hero." Steve, himself a veteran, felt the injustice as both a father and a soldier.

"When I first learned that the man who had raped my daughter would be granted a military honors burial, I couldn't grasp that this could be our government's policy," says Steve. "It was such an affront to victims, and to good veterans, men and women who deserve to be buried alongside other heroes, not criminals. So I was very angry. But this was not political for me, not at first. I approached this as a father who wanted to protect my daughter from more hurt and protect other people's daughters from ever going through this. The issue was bigger than Jenny, but at the same time it was all about Jenny for me. Her courage and resilience inspired me. "

Steve, a healthcare entrepreneur, is a problem solver by trade. So he set out to solve the problem. With Jenny's encouragement—she says she was "so honored that my dad cared this much and so proud that he wanted to do this"—Steve started learning about the issue of rape in the US military and the consequences, or lack thereof, for those who commit it. He met with victim and veterans groups, raising awareness of the need for a change in military burials policy. He joined the board of End Violence Against Women International to become engaged in the day-to-day struggle to end gender-based violence. And Steve began talking to national advocacy organizations, strategizing with them about how to turn his outrage into a bill, and that bill into Jenny's Law.

If Jenny is the bill's inspiration, Steve is very much its engine. It has been his outreach that has raised national awareness of the need for a change in policy. Watching Steve meet with members of the House and Senate and their staffs—as I did when I spent a day with him as he lobbied for Jenny's Law on Capitol Hill—is deeply moving. It is also difficult to witness, because there are times when, as he shares Jenny's story, Steve's eyes cloud in that same way they did the first time I met him. But they clear again as he speaks with conviction, makes his case for the law, and then moves on to the next congressional office. "Jenny and the other women who testified against Selby are the heroes here," says Steve. "They are the ones who took a serial rapist off the street. When I think about that, going office to office on Capitol Hill seems like a very small thing."

In the made-for-TV version of Jenny and Steve's story, Jenny's Law would have passed years ago. In the real world, realpolitik has intruded, and the bill—which has not yet come up for a vote in the US Senate—will need to be reintroduced during the next Congress. "I was naïve, in retrospect," Steve says. "I imagined this bill becoming a law within the year, with people on the left and right coming together on it. But this law has not yet had a really impassioned advocate on the Hill, and there has been resistance to Jenny's Law from veterans groups. There are people on the Hill who won't support anything that can be seen as anti-military. Of course, I'm a veteran, and to me this law is pro-military: it would guarantee that a good solider would never be buried alongside a criminal in one of our national cemeteries. But let's be honest: there are not a lot of areas right now where the military is doing the right thing for victims of rape."

It is the summer of 2013 as I write this, and Steve's statement about the military and its response to rape victims is devastatingly accurate. The US Department of Defense estimates that more than nineteen thousand sexual assaults occurred in the armed services in 2010; fewer than 14 percent of those assaults were ever reported to authorities. And recent studies show that unwanted sexual contact in the ranks increased 35 percent from 2010 to 2012. By any standard, this is not only a crisis—it's an epidemic.

Military and sexual aggression have been linked since the earliest accounts of battle, according to Helen Benedict, the groundbreaking journalist who wrote *The Lonely Solider*, an exposé of rape in the US military. "It's pre-biblical if you go to the Greeks and even earlier—the idea of women as being loot, or 'booty,'" Benedict said in a 2013 *Huffington Post* interview. "The idea that conquering soldiers are entitled to help themselves to women's bodies is as ancient as the idea of the soldier itself. So that is very deep within every military in the world."

This has devastating consequences not just for enlisted women but also for women who interact with soldiers and veterans in civilian life. A soldier who rapes while serving in the military will almost surely rape again once he is outside of it. As is the case with the civilian population, rates of recidivism are high among sex offenders.

Jenny's is only one story, and a unique one in many ways. Given the small number of veterans ever convicted of rape, passage of Jenny's Law will affect relatively few people. Yet the fact that such a policy is needed at all serves as a symbol and symptom of a US military that responds inadequately—and sometimes not at all—to the sexual violence committed by those in its ranks.

It is tempting, and far too easy, to maintain that the military exists in a realm separate from the civilian world. But the argument made by those who resist reform of the military's policies on sexual violence—that the moral ambiguities demonstrated by soldiers cannot be understood by, or be subject to, the laws that govern the rest of us—becomes less convincing each year. The truth is that the policies our military establishes to respond to violence against women are not merely abstractions. They are expressions of the military's values and our national will. And they must change.

Steve Bush is well aware of this. "I came into this thinking about Jenny, and I still think of what she lived through, every day. The sad thing is that Jenny is one of the lucky ones. She survived, she testified, she has rebuilt her life, and she has had support from her family every step of the way. But for every Jenny out there, there are hundreds of women who never see anything close to justice. Jenny is the exception, not the rule."

The Advocate: **Tracey Stevens**

Tracey Stevens loves problems (because she is a problem solver), disorder (because she is an organizer), and questions (because no one thrills to the search for an answer more than she does). She is a legal secretary at Winston & Strawn LLP, one of the country's largest law firms, and she will tell you, completely without irony, that "God is in the details." Where you or I see a desk laden with documents, Tracey sees a perfect filing system waiting to happen.

Tracey doesn't tell me any of this when we meet for the first time. She doesn't have to. Instead, minutes after we exchange greetings and sit down on a city park bench not far from the downtown high-rise where she works, Tracey takes a thick legal file folder out of her tote bag, opens it carefully to reveal stacks of documents, and indicates to me that she is ready to talk. When a stray gust of Lake Michigan wind threatens to blow a page away, she gently—almost lovingly—presses her right palm down so that everything remains in order. Over the course of the next few hours, that file folder rarely leaves Tracey's lap.

The documents it holds tell a story—Tracey's story—in official language and Helvetica type. As she takes me through these pages, which include correspondence related to the 1997 trial of the man who sexually assaulted her, health insurance claim forms filed during the months after she was attacked, and years of letters written to a Michigan parole board, I can feel Tracey's pain. But even more than that, I can feel her pride: *This is what happened to me. This is what it cost me. This is what I have done to reclaim my life.*

Tracey was twenty-five years old when she was sexually assaulted in the shower at a public campground in Michigan. Her boyfriend Greg's family had a trailer there, and it had always been one of her favorite places: safe, peaceful, and beautiful. Tracey, Greg, and a few of their friends were relaxing around the campfire at the end of a June day spent boating and fishing. "I can't remember much about that day, except that it was normal," says Tracey. "Later on, I would think about how amazing just having a 'normal' day was."

Tracey decided to call it a night at 10:00 p.m. and headed to the campground shower to clean up before going to bed. She had been showering for a few minutes when she heard the rings of the shower curtain slide back. She started, turned, and saw a large man wearing a blue ski mask moving toward her. For Tracey, that moment was life altering. "Honestly, even if he had turned and walked away, I was so terrified that I knew I would never be the same again," she says.

He didn't walk away. The man was large—over two hundred pounds—and he had a roll of duct tape in his hand. He slammed it repeatedly into Tracey's head to subdue her, as he grabbed her breasts and genital area and unzipped his pants. Tracey fought back, kicking and screaming as loud as she could.

Resisting was not an instinct for Tracey—it was a considered decision. "It sounds crazy and almost wrong to use the word 'just' with rape," she says. "But honestly, my first thought was, if I just let him rape me, will that keep him from killing me? But my gut told me that I needed to fight." When her assailant momentarily stopped hitting and groping Tracey and tried to tape her mouth shut, Tracey screamed a final time.

Tracey's attacker fled as Tracey's friends and other campground guests raced toward the scene. Tracey's boyfriend, Greg, followed the attacker as he ran into the woods. Tracey, who had come out of the shower in search of help, was in shock. She says of those first moments after she broke free, "I was crying, naked, and I remember that soap was running in my eyes and burning, but I couldn't care less." When Greg came back to tell Tracey they had caught the man who assaulted her, she remembers her relief. "I had no idea anyone even heard me screaming."

"I do remember thinking that it was funny that I was standing nude in a public place and not minding that at all," Tracey says. "All that mattered was that I was alive." A camper who was a nurse took Tracey back inside the women's bathroom and helped her get dressed. The police arrived within minutes, arrested Tracey's assailant, and took statements from Tracey and the other witnesses. "You kind of piece those first hours together later, as people tell you what you said and did," Tracey says. "It's hard to remember it all yourself."

Tracey and Greg returned to Greg's Indiana apartment early that morning. The next day they went to a local hospital so that Tracey could be given a complete medical examination. Tracey was badly bruised, aching, and swollen, but the wound she recalls most clearly from that day was dealt her by the X-ray technician who checked her for broken bones. It was her first brush with official indifference, or at least ineptitude, and the memory still stings. "He asked me what happened, and I told him that I had been sexually assaulted," says Tracey. "He stared at me, didn't express any sympathy at all, and sort of shrugged and said, 'Well, it could have been worse. At least you're alive.'"

"It was less than a day after I was attacked, and at that time I felt more hurt than angry," says Tracey. "Now when I think about it, I get so pissed. Sexual assault and 'it could have been worse' should never be in the same sentence."

For Tracey, returning to her "normal life" was difficult. She loved her job as a legal secretary, her daily commute to the city, and the energy of working in a bustling downtown office. Suddenly, all of that felt overwhelming. "Part of me wanted to curl up into a ball at Greg's and just stay there for good," says Tracey. "I was so depressed that I was practically immobile. I was too scared to go back to my apartment and live alone. But I had to get back to my life, or that monster would have won. "

Tracey took a week off to allow her black eye and the most visible bruises to heal. She was almost never alone during that time—her sisters, parents, and boyfriend were constantly with her. But on the following Monday, nine days after she had been sexually assaulted, she set her alarm for 5:00 a.m., put on a long-sleeved blouse and "lots of concealer," and headed back to work.

Tracey had told the human resources department at her law firm that she was sexually assaulted, and she also informed the two attorneys she worked most closely with. They agreed to tell Tracey's colleagues that she had been in a bad car accident, which would explain her bruises.

Tracey makes clear that she felt "absolutely no shame" about having been sexually assaulted. She just wasn't ready to talk about what had happened to her at work. "It's odd to think of now, because today, almost everyone at the firm who works with me knows I'm a rape survivor," says Tracey. "But going back was hard enough without having to talk about what had just happened to me. I needed to do that when I was ready, and not before."

Still, Tracey was grateful that a handful of colleagues were aware that she had been sexually assaulted. Her boss Cathy—a partner at the firm whom Tracey admires deeply and is very close to—was one of those people. "Cathy knew how hard this was, and in little ways she would let me know that she understood," Tracey says. "Sometimes she would just say, 'Tracey, go outside and get some fresh air,' no matter how much work I had to do."

Work was in many ways an oasis for Tracey: eight hours a day, when her busy schedule distracted her from her depression and anger. But even in the safety of her forty-fourth-floor office, she sometimes felt anxiety. "If someone came up behind me to ask me a question, I would suddenly start or flinch," Tracey says. "It felt awful to have that flashback, and it made me so self-conscious"

Tracey says that she had never before been a fearful person—"I have always been very tough and strong, your best friend and your worst enemy"—but seemingly overnight, all of that had changed. She became anxious in crowds. She developed stress-related stomach issues. She experienced waves of panic that left her exhausted at the end of each day.

Showering—even in the safety of Greg's home—was terrifying for Tracey, unless Greg stayed in the bathroom with her. "He spent a lot of nights and mornings sitting on the floor outside his shower," she remembers. "Thank God for Greg. I don't know how clean I would have been that first year without that," she laughs.

Still, it was nighttime that was most difficult for Tracey. She was often too anxious to sleep, despite her fatigue. When she finally drifted off—usually with the help of the anti-anxiety medication that got her through those first few months—Tracey would have nightmares and wake screaming. "It was classic posttraumatic stress disorder, although I knew nothing about that at the time," Tracey says. "I just felt like my whole life had been turned upside down, and I wanted the old me back."

Antidepressants and counseling helped, but Tracey believes that even with that kind of support, recovery takes time. "You can't expect everything to go back to normal after this," she says. "Expecting that a pill or a therapist will make you 'snap out of it' will just lead you to more disappointment. You heal on your own schedule."

Tracey shares details of the first year after she was sexually assaulted matter-of-factly. She does not cry, she does not hesitate, and she uses very few adjectives when talking about her physical and emotional symptoms. She says that in many ways talking about what happened to her is more difficult than it is therapeutic for her. But she does it because she believes it is important for other survivors to understand that the recovery process is complicated.

"Some people think that sexual assault is a one-time event, but for me it was an event followed by lots of physical and emotional changes that just kept happening," says Tracey. "If I had known that at the time, I could have felt more 'normal.' Because feeling crazy for a while actually *is* normal after rape."

Tracey remembers every act of kindness that she experienced during those first few months after she was sexually assaulted: the friend who brought over her favorite ice cream because he was worried that she had lost her appetite, the way that the gift of the book *When Bad Things Happen To Good People* made her cry, the hugs that her nephew gave her when he sensed her sadness.

"People had been good to me before I was raped," says Tracey. "But when you are feeling so vulnerable, those moments someone reaches out to you are burned in your memory. They will always be some of the most important moments of my life."

The trial of Tracey's assailant occurred eight months after she was attacked. The disconnect between how Tracey felt at that time—"my whole life had been turned upside down, and I was still struggling"—and the way that the defense presented what her assailant had done was striking.

"If you listened to his defense attorney talk about the crime, you could summarize it with three words: 'No big deal,'" says Tracey. "The man who sexually assaulted me told the court-appointed doctor who evaluated him that he just wanted to 'touch my tits' and 'have a little fun.' To know that the most terrifying event of my life was being called 'fun'—it made me so angry."

"At one point during the trial, the defense attorney actually asked me why I was showering naked—sort of implying that I must have been asking for this to happen," says Tracey. "I mean, come on! How else do you shower? It seemed ridiculous at first, but they badger you and bully you, and you're seated just a few feet away from the person who did all of this to you. I was so angry that I just broke down and cried on the stand."

Tracey turns again to her file at this point in our conversation. She pulls out a psychiatric evaluation of the man who sexually assaulted her, a document that was submitted by the defense at his sentencing. And she directs my attention to the conclusion, which states that her attacker is "not malicious" and "just wants to find his place in the world and achieve a level of security and happiness." Those two words still rankle Tracey: "Security and happiness. For a long time, he took all of that from me, and more."

Tracey read a victim impact statement at the trial, detailing for the court and the man who had attacked her how his actions had affected her. "I was lucky because I researched it, and I knew how important that victim impact statement could be," says Tracey. "So I took a lot of time to look at everything that had happened during the year: how I had changed, what new medical bills I had, all of the time I spent seeing doctors, or a counselor, or going without sleep. I went over every receipt and record and spelled it out for the court. I didn't want them to miss anything."

Tracey's assailant never made eye contact with her as she read her victim impact statement. He never contested his guilt and never expressed any remorse. On February 24, 1997, he was convicted of criminal sexual conduct and assault with intent to commit sexual penetration. He was sentenced to one year in jail and ten years' probation.

I ask Tracey if she felt safer during the year that the man who sexually assaulted her was locked up. "Yes and no," she says. "This specific man could not hurt me. But after you are raped, you never feel safe again. He was locked up, but that does not mean that I was free."

Tracey's assailant was released in 1998. Less than a year later, he was caught outside another woman's home, looking in her window as she showered. Having violated the terms of his parole, he was sent back to prison. Tracey remembers exactly what she felt when she learned that he had been stalking a second victim. "Horrible for her," says Tracey, "and outraged that he was given the chance to do this again."

What Tracey did not feel was shock. "The defense had argued that I was 'just' his first victim, so they should go easy on him and not put him away for too long," says Tracey. "After this happened to me, I spent a lot of time researching sex crimes and how often rapists are repeat offenders. I realized that I probably wasn't his first victim. I was just the first·victim he got caught attacking. Once he got out, I was sure he would do it again, and he did. Because men who rape do not stop. Victims know that. It just seems like the legal system doesn't."

Tracey had gained strength during the three years that followed her attack. She and Greg married in 1997—he proposed to Tracey six months after she was sexually assaulted—and their relationship was a key source of her confidence. Her day-to-day panic attacks had lessened as well. "I would say that by that third year I had pretty much woven the sexual assault into the rest of my life," Tracey says. "I felt powerful again. There was no doubt that I was going to fight it when he was up for parole again."

To prepare for that fight, Tracey went into legal secretary mode. She kept a calendar of every key date related to her perpetrator's case and his parole hearings. She kept copious files of key contacts at the Michigan Department of Corrections. She did her homework and reviewed legal briefs and letters that had swayed other parole boards. And she wrote. And wrote. And wrote.

Tracey's letters to the Michigan Department of Corrections Prisoner Review Board, arguing against the parole of the man who had sexually assaulted her, were sent annually between the years of 1997 and 2008. Neatly organized in her legal file folder, the letters are quintessential Tracey: impassioned, practical, and direct (not to mention copiously spell-checked).

Tracey had one goal: keeping the man who had attacked her locked up for as long as the law would allow. "I basically told the parole board, 'Look what he did to me, and don't think for a minute that he won't do it again,'" Tracey says. "I did not want them to be able to say 'We couldn't have known; no one told us.'"

Tracey had become familiar enough with the legal system to understand that the content of her letters mattered. But she believes that the fact that they were being written at all was just as important. "You want members of the parole board to know that someone is paying attention," Tracey says. "You want them to realize that if this monster gets out and does this again, someone will be saying, 'You are responsible.' Because no one wants to be responsible for a crime that could have been avoided."

Tracey is proud of her efforts. But she is candid about the fact that her multi-year letter-writing campaign was at times more difficult than it was rewarding. Each year she was distracted, painfully, by two key dates: the June anniversary of her sexual assault and the annual parole hearing of her assailant. "You want to move on," says Tracey. "But you have to keep going back. But I would do it again if it helped one other woman avoid what I went through."

Addressing the systemic problem of light sentences for sexual predators will take more than a letter-writing campaign, and Tracey knows it. "What I did only kept one man locked up for a few extra years—he was released in 2008, and he is free today," she says. "But there are millions of other men like him out there."

Only three out of every one hundred rapists will ever spend even a single day in prison, according to a 2013 analysis of Justice Department data done by RAINN. The other ninety-seven will walk free, facing no legal or civil consequences for the felonies they have committed. These are figures that represent an injustice to victims like Tracey and a risk to the general public, as serial predators remain free to rape and abuse again.

Even when sexual predators do serve time, their sentences can be shockingly short. According to a US Department of Justice study published in 1995, the average sentence for convicted rapists was 11.8 years, while the actual time served was 5.4 years. For most rape and sexual assault victims, these figures are both stunning and heartbreaking. "Men who rape and abuse are thieves," says Tracey. "They steal our peace of mind, our feeling of being safe, and the lives we had before. And then they get a slap on the wrist for it, and that's so wrong."

Working to right that wrong has become a mission for Tracey. In 2004, she began speaking out about her story through her work with the Voices and Faces Project. "I wanted to hold my head high and say, 'Yes, this happened to me, and very little was done to stop it from happening to the next woman,' says Tracey. "And I wanted to stand with other survivors and help them talk about their stories, too. Because none of us have anything to hide."

Today, Tracey doesn't just share her own story. She also brings her legal skills to bear on behalf of other victims. In 2006, she approached her law firm, Winston and Strawn, about providing pro bono legal support to other members of the Voices and Faces Project who choose to share their stories of surviving sexual violence with the public or the media. Tracey serves as the liaison between the law firm and the nonprofit organization, and she says that making that connection possible is something she is most proud of.

"Some of my coworkers started out wanting to help because they knew I was a survivor," says Tracey. "But over time, when people learned about the facts around rape and abuse, I think they started to realize that it is a huge problem in our country," says Tracey.

Tracey says that she will never stop talking about her experience. For her, the pain of sexual violence has faded, but the power of her story has not.

"I share my story because I want other survivors to know that the bad days are not going to last forever," says Tracey. "The fear fades. But the anger lives on. And that's OK, because a little anger can do a lot of good."

New Rules for Radicals

I had been waiting for this man all of my life, so of course I fell head over heels when I finally encountered him. I loved his Jewish humor. I thrilled, as only a good Methodist girl can, to his bad-boy propensity for citing Lucifer, whom he considered history's first great rebel. I even forgave him his relative indifference to women's issues and his chain-smoking ways (a virtuous man must have at least one vice to be bearable).

I loved him for a dozen reasons, but mostly I loved him because he helped me make a sort of moral sense of my own worldview. He taught me that my ability to assimilate might—*might*—be wise instead of weak, if I chose to use that ability for the good. He convinced me that I could engage in radical acts while wearing four-inch heels (the better with which to be underestimated, my dear). He showed me that using words and stories that pull people in, instead of pushing them away, could open hearts and minds in a way that angry confrontation sometimes can't. Make people feel, he instructed me, and then you can get them to act.

His name was Saul Alinsky. I never met him—when he died of a massive heart attack in 1972, I was just seven years old. But years later, when I discovered his groundbreaking third book, *Rules for*

Radicals: A Pragmatic Primer for Realistic Radicals, it didn't so much change my worldview as challenge me to act on that worldview in a new way.

Alinsky is sui generis, an activist who is widely considered the founder of modern community organizing, and *Rules for Radicals* is a blueprint for anyone interested in changing public opinion or public policy. Alinsky's reach has been long and wide. Hillary Rodham Clinton wrote her Wellesley senior honors thesis about the man, and President Obama was inspired enough by Alinsky's teachings to follow in his Chicago community-organizing footsteps, a fact that briefly made headlines during the 2012 presidential campaign (the words "radical" and "President Obama" being too irresistible a combination for Fox News to resist).

Alinsky was a radical in the true and most noble sense of the word—he wanted real change, in real time, and he believed that the fight for the poor, the marginalized, and the maligned depended on it. But beliefs are not the subject of *Rules for Radicals*. Tactics are. In the world according to Saul Alinsky, the desire to change things is good. But the ability to change things is, in the end, what matters.

No contemporary corporate CEO bandies about the idea of "getting results" with more relish than does Alinsky. He was a realist, but more than that he was a strategist—someone who believed that we work, and think, our way to change. He makes clear, over and over again, that passion must be paired with pragmatism to matter much at all. "Start from where the world is, as it is," he implores his readers. "It is necessary to begin where the world is if we are going to change it to what we think it should be."

Alinsky made clear over the course of his organizing career that outside agitators can play a critical role in transforming our world. But in *Rules for Radicals*, he also makes an impassioned case for pursuing transformation from within the system, where the vast majority of Americans live and breathe.

Long before journalist Malcolm Gladwell was talking about "connectors"—those rare individuals who manage to move effortlessly between different worlds, bringing together people and ideologies—Alinsky was reminding us that one of the most radical acts we can engage in is bridge building. Moving people from "the security of familiar experience to a new way" is, for Alinsky, both noble and necessary.

The pragmatics of change have long fascinated me. I grew up in a small town so resistant to time's progressive arrow that subversion seemed to me to be the best, and certainly the most immediately available, option for challenging the status quo.

I became convinced of this while watching my father rage against the suburban machine in a more overt way. He was a leftist and environmentalist who relished the fact that he had been blacklisted by the John Birch Society (we were never quite sure if this was true, those pesky blacklists being difficult to find in the pre-digital era). He read voraciously and, with facts on his side, engaged in political discussions with a sort of myopic passion—no debater has ever been less aware of his audience than my father was. He wore his ideology the way he wore faded and patched Levi's to a picnic where khakis were de rigueur, with the sort of defiance that is charming in the abstract—I'm smiling as I write this—but usually off-putting in real life. You always saw my father and his antibusiness, pro-environment politics coming, which gave people plenty of time to fortify their defenses against him.

I could not have been more than ten or eleven at the time, but I still remember my mother rushing upstairs to the playroom where a group of our friends had congregated during an adult party hosted by one of our neighbors. "Ream children, we have to go now! Your father is fighting about the environment again," she exclaimed. I could feel her embarrassment and mild panic, and I felt embarrassed, too. It wasn't my father's arguing over eco-issues that troubled me. In my young mind, I was certain that he must have right on his side to annoy people as he did. It was his inability to win the fight. He fashioned himself as a noble insider, but he was an inefficient one as well. I don't think I ever saw him change someone's mind.

My mother lacked my father's ideological fervor but believed just as deeply in "doing the right thing." If my father was a matchstick, my mother was the blanket, eager to snuff out a potential political blaze by insisting that we all "wanted the same thing" and just needed to find "common ground." Those two phrases are also lovely in the abstract. But in real life they obscure the fact that robust disagreement (of the respectful variety) is critical to change. "Change means movement. Movement means friction," Alinsky argued, around the time that my mother was dragging her brood out of that neighborhood party.

The key question, of course, is what kind of friction is most likely to lead to lasting social change. And whether there are other paths to transformation that might not depend on friction (of the readily apparent variety) at all.

Here's the empowering, and possibly uncomfortable, truth: most of us have been outsourcing the ability to create change for far too long. We look to politicians or activists or the "chattering classes" to move the needle on issues that matter to us. What we really need to do is look at ourselves. So henceforth, a modest proposal for creating a set of "New Rules for Radicals"—a proposal grounded in what I'll call the three s's: Storytelling, Opinion Shaping, and, perhaps most importantly, Subversion.

Let's start with the power of stories—our own, and those of other people. No effective social movement has ever existed without them. It was Rosa Parks's 1955 refusal to give up her seat to a white bus passenger that gave birth to the contemporary civil rights movement, launched the Montgomery bus boycott, and brought a then-unknown minister named Martin Luther King Jr. to the attention of mainstream America.

It was the 1998 slaying of Matthew Shepard, a young gay man from Laramie, Wyoming, that galvanized support for hate crimes legislation, putting a name and a face on the violence far too many gay and lesbian youth, and adults, have endured.

It was thousands of mothers, speaking out about the heartbreak of losing their children to drunk drivers, which led to the creation of Mothers Against Drunk Drivers (MADD) and a new set of legal and social norms. Today, it's difficult to imagine a time when drinking and driving were seen as normal, not criminal (though *Mad Men*, that time capsule in the form of a TV show, makes it possible).

The stories at the center of these cultural shifts did not singularly make the argument for change. In each of these cases, the need for a new order was already blowing insistently in the wind. But these stories made change feel urgent and essential, reminding us that it was time—past time—that we acted on what we knew.

There is a growing body of contemporary research that puts a fine point on the power of storytelling. In *Redirect: The Surprising Science of Psychological Change*, University of Virginia psychology professor Timothy Wilson posits that stories are more important than data when it comes to changing minds, hearts, and even public policies, allowing us to emotionally identify with those we might previously have seen as "outsiders." Once we see bits and pieces of ourselves in another person's story, it becomes increasingly difficult to turn away from their needs or suffering.

We like to think of ourselves and our world as rational. We are often wrong. "It is useless to reason a man out of what he was never reasoned into," satirist Jonathan Swift pithily wrote, over two centuries before Professor Wilson embarked on his research. Put another way, our attitudes are products of the stories we've been told since we were young—by our families, our peers, our communities, our places of worship, and (especially as regards gender-based violence) our media. To change those attitudes, we must create a whole new set of narratives, thinking of story sharing as a strategic, and not only cathartic, exercise.

The Rosa Parks example is instructive. Her refusal to give up that seat on the bus looms so large in American history that it has largely obscured the fact that her fateful decision was not spontaneous, but considered. Rosa Parks had been carefully selected by the NAACP as the public face around which to build a case for bus desegregation, after two other candidates were deemed less prepared for the media's glare.

"Look at the photographs of Rosa Parks throughout her life, and at the time that she was arrested for not giving up her seat on that Montgomery bus," says historian Danielle McGuire, the author of *At the Dark End of the Street: Black Women, Rape, and Resistance—A New History of the Civil Rights Movement from Rosa Parks to the Rise of Black Power*. "There was something überpure about the way that she presented herself. Rosa Parks was a deeply committed activist and, at the same time, very 'media savvy,' long before that phrase was used. She had a lifelong understanding of the power of image in the battle for civil rights."

None of this obscures the fact that Rosa Parks's refusal to give up her seat was heroic or heartfelt. But it shows us that Parks and her NAACP colleagues understood that they were telling a story, and they wanted to tell it in the way that would engage the largest possible audience. It reminds us that strategy and ideology can (and perhaps must) co-exist.

Our use of language is also critical to our storytelling efforts. In a 2006 paper on media bias, University of Chicago economists Jesse Shapiro and Matthew Gentzgow posit that there are words and terms that "cue" ideology and are most often used by those on the Right or Left. Being aware of such words—and knowing when it may be most effective to embrace or refrain from using them—is critical to reaching people "where they are."

This is something that Reverend King seemed to instinctively understand. King—unlike the generation of civil right leaders that had come before him—rarely used the word *equality* (it only appears once in his legendary "I Have a Dream" speech). Instead, he spoke eloquently, passionately, and often about *freedom*, a term that is as universal and inclusive as any in the English language. He read his audience carefully and used language that reflected their needs, values, hopes, and, of course, dreams.

Effective storytelling can take many forms in our media-driven era. In 2006, researchers from Ohio State University and Colorado State University conducted a study on how exposure to an issue-oriented TV drama can change attitudes, regardless of the viewer's political affiliation. They split 178 students into two groups: the first group watched an expertly produced true crime program that reinforced arguments in favor of the death penalty; the second watched an unrelated drama. After viewing these two programs, the researchers interviewed the students about their beliefs on capital punishment. The students who watched the true crime show were more likely to support the death penalty, regardless of whether they identified as liberal or conservative. Among the students who watched the "neutral" program, support for the death penalty was most strongly predicted by political ideology (liberals opposed, conservative supported).

Here's what that research, and likely our own experience, tell us: nothing breaks through ideological barriers quite so forcefully as a well-told story. Mia Goldman understands this well. She comes from a family of award-winning filmmakers, and she's spent most of her life editing and directing. Mia was raped on a film set in 1989, an event that changed her in ways she "never could have anticipated." In 2006 she turned her filmmaker's lens on that experience, writing and directing *Open Window*, a Sundance Film Festival selection that explores rape and its aftermath for the victim and those who are closest to her. "Film is my vocabulary, so that is how I wanted to tell my story," says Mia.

To talk to Mia is to know that she has strong beliefs about gender-based violence and our public policies on rape. To watch *Open Window* is to see those beliefs woven seamlessly into a story that engages as it educates. As Saul Alinsky might observe, Mia did more than make a film. She built a bridge to a new audience.

Mia Goldman

Our stories are inherently powerful—and they are made more so when we bring them to the attention of the largest possible audience. This is why opinion shapers are so important.

Speaking to those who can most immediately effect change—the policymakers, faith-based leaders, and community influencers who wield unique power within the institutions with which they are affiliated—is critical to any strategic storytelling effort. All men and women are created equal, but their ability to exert influence is anything but. We ignore this truth at our peril.

I saw this theory in action when the organization with which I am affiliated, the Voices and Faces Project, engaged in an outreach program in partnership with Pastor Jon Ireland, the charismatic leader of Ocean Hills Covenant Church in Santa Barbara, California.

Pastor Ireland is a New Testament-quoting, outdoor-adventure-loving surfer. He ministers to a largely privileged congregation but says that he feels called to "acknowledge blessings while challenging social injustices." He is by nature and sometimes by choice an optimist—*awesome* is one of his favorite words. Pastor Ireland is exuberant, but he is also serious, which is why he decided to create an entire Sunday morning service focused on gender-based violence, something I had not seen done before.

So we worked together to introduce his congregation to the stories of survivors through a slide show featuring photos taken by Voices and Faces Project photographer Patricia Evans. Pastor Ireland read and listened and learned from members of our organization before crafting a sermon that denounced gender-based violence as morally wrong and inconsistent with Christian teaching. At the end of the Ocean Hills Sunday service, he invited me to the front of his church to take part in a candid, freewheeling Q&A—one in which he and I talked about the ways that faith-based communities were falling short, how to create a church environment where victims feel supported, and the limitations of forgiveness.

Looking out into that Sunday morning crowd of over four hundred parishioners and speaking out with—and not just to—Pastor Ireland felt vital and new to me. This is what "meeting people where they are" means.

Pastor Ireland is an institutional opinion shaper who had the courage and creativity to use his position of leadership to create change from within. He shakes things up, gently—but the important thing is that he shakes.

I witnessed a similar sort of opinion shaping when I watched Marina Nemat, the author of *Prisoner of Tehran: One Woman's Story of Survival in an Iranian Prison*, a memoir of surviving rape and torture during the Islamic Revolution, speak at Stand Up for Women, an event hosted by Fairbanks Republican Women Federated, one of the country's oldest and most venerated Republican women's groups.

Marina is a petite, soft-spoken, extraordinarily gentle presence who opened her talk by recalling how, growing up in Tehran, her great love was the Laura Ingalls Wilder Little House on the Prairie books (audience connection: immediate). But she did not stay in that rhetorical safe zone for long. Instead, she moved on to share the details of her story. To watch Marina decry torture in front of more than four hundred largely—though not exclusively—conservative activists in San Diego County, California, was to see a woman afforded her stature through one thing: the expression of her truth.

When she used her story to make the moral, political, and practical case against the use of torture by the United States and any other government that values human rights, an awed hush overcame the room. It may have been the silence of sympathy or discomfort or even disagreement, but one thing was certain: people were listening. The standing ovation that Marina received when she finished her remarks was long and enthusiastic.

Marina made her way into that room through Stephanie Hanson, an activist who serves on the executive director's Leadership Council of Amnesty International, the Nobel Prize–winning human rights organization. Stephanie, a moderate Republican who believes human rights and women's rights should not be the exclusive purview of either political party, is accustomed to straddling disparate and often mutually distrusting worlds. As a survivor of sexual violence—and an outspoken voice condemning torture and other human rights violations—she sometimes finds herself at odds with members of her own party. "I can argue about the facts on human rights issues," Stephanie says, "or I can introduce people who don't get it to someone like Marina." The Stand Up for Women event was Stephanie's brainchild—her way of contributing to a substantive dialogue about social justice issues that includes people on the Right and the Left.

I am not naïve enough to believe that Marina changed every mind in the room during that public forum. Logic would dictate that if she moved the needle with her story—at least among those who are convinced that torture is a "necessary evil," and the Violence Against Women Act "feminist pork"—it was incrementally. But incremental change still matters, and Marina's resolutely political, insistently non-partisan words reminded the audience that the concept of human rights shouldn't belong to a single party. It belongs to every person with a conscience.

Having made the moral case for storytelling, and the practical case for the power of opinion shapers like Jon Ireland, Marina Nemat, and Stephanie Hanson, let's turn—at last—to the subversives.

Is there a more beautiful word in the English language? *Subversion* is a promise that the old order is waiting to give way to something better, if only we dare to upend it. It's a reminder that we can ask for change, and negotiate endlessly in service to it, but there are times when we have no choice but to demand it.

Subversion is the righteous anger of Jaclyn Friedman, Soraya Chemaly, and Laura Bates. Frustrated by Facebook's tolerance of misogynist hate speech on its pages—and convinced that the best way to encourage the company to take action was through the power of the pocketbook—they created an online protest campaign that generated over five thousand e-mails and sixty thousand posts on Twitter, alerting advertisers and the general public to Facebook's failure to keep their online space safe. It was a campaign that prompted Nissan, and more than a dozen smaller companies that advertise on Facebook, to threaten to pull their advertising from the social networking site if the company didn't commit to changing its policies (it did). The beauty of this effort lay in its simplicity: bring to light policies that threaten a corporation's image and its revenue stream—they are, of course, linked—and things can change very quickly.

The effectiveness of the campaign is also evidence—with apologies to Audre Lorde—that sometimes the master's tools *can* be

Jaclyn Friedman

used to dismantle the master's house. This irony is not lost on Jaclyn Friedman, a cap-F feminist, schooled in more traditional forms of protest. The issue of misogynist speech online is one that is both personal and political for her. "Look, as a rape survivor, when I see a Facebook page that glorifies rape, of course I'm pissed and shocked," says Jaclyn. "How is it that in 2013 this is still going on? But you work with what you have, and turning social media on itself, using Facebook to demand that Facebook stop tolerating hate speech— that gave us real power."

Change is the result of a chorus, not a solo. It happens when an injustice feels so real and so wrong that many people—often very different people—feel compelled to engage in the fight to end it. It occurs when we look at the world, find it lacking, and then look at ourselves and ask, "What can I do?" It emerges when we use what we have—something as large-scale as a social network, or as intimate as a one-on-one conversation—to make a righteous demand. And radical action—smart, creative, radical action—is most possible when we listen as carefully as we talk, hearing the stories of other women and amplifying them with our own voices.

My own philosophy of change is evolving. I've spent much of my life living and working within systems, pushing hard—some might say too hard—for change from inside. But the truth is that no matter how hard one is pushing, *inside* is by definition the safe side. The real wilderness is over there, not in here.

This is a lesson that I've learned from watching my friend Helen Benedict, a Columbia University journalism professor and the author of *The Lonely Soldier: The Private War of Women in Iraq*. The book— and her reporting on sexual violence against female soldiers committed by men in the ranks—served as the inspiration for *The Invisible War*, the Academy Award–nominated documentary that brought the epidemic of soldier-on-soldier sexual violence to the attention of the general public, and resulted in an ongoing lawsuit against the Pentagon on behalf of soldiers who were sexually assaulted while serving their country.

Today, an acknowledgment of that "invisible war" is so complete that military-based sexual violence is one of the few areas where bipartisanship remains possible, as evidenced by the collaboration between Republican senator Rand Paul and Democratic senator Kirsten Gillibrand, who came together in July 2013 to call for a new military prosecution system for those who commit sex crimes.

But in 2006, when Helen began writing *The Lonely Soldier*, she was rather lonely herself. She was one of the first, and certainly one of the most insistent, voices decrying the military's failure to protect female soldiers from the men they were serving with. Helen remembers being called a "liar" and an "exaggerator" during the early days of making her claims. She didn't set out to expose the epidemic of sexual violence in the military. She sought to simply tell the stories of five female soldiers. Listening to them brought to light a world where soldier-on-soldier rape was frequent, and perpetrators were most often provided impunity. She didn't so much tell a story as follow it.

Does Helen relish confrontation? I'm not sure. But she knows that it is necessary. She is angry (because, having heard the stories of too many female soldiers who have been raped, she should be). She is impatient (because she has heard *this will be the year, finally, at last, when we make things right* one time too many). She often distrusts the motives of those working for change from within (because if experience has taught Helen anything, it's that even good-faith players can go bad in a failing system).

Helen may not be right about the solutions to the problem of military-based sexual violence—there are plenty of conflicting opinions on where to go next. What she is right about, and what she has been right about for years, is the existence and extent of the problem. Her willingness to tell a story that the world—and certainly the US military—did not want to hear was transformative for millions of women. That is legacy.

So a final case—inspired by Helen—for creating a bit of discomfort (your own, and someone else's). Don't fear it too much. Being willing to "afflict the comfortable" doesn't mean that you've stopped caring—it means you've started caring about the right things. What happens after you do that can change everything.

PHOTOGRAPHY BY NATALIE NACCACHE, FROM THE ART WORKS FOR CHANGE AWARE/OWARE
PROJECT

Impassioned: **Sister Fa**

"I want my girls to be happy and kind," my mother would often say to me, and on the face of it, who could argue with her? Happiness and kindness were states that generations of women in my family had aspired to, as evidenced by the ancient framed embroidery still hanging on the walls of the guestroom in her home. "Cheerfulness breeds harmony," reads one, in meticulous cross-stitch, and "Contentment is happiness," the other. "What, no 'Happiness is a warm gun' to complete the trifecta?" a friend who stayed in the room once laughed. He had a point.

I think of those embroidered admonitions when I think about Sister Fa (proper name: Fatou Diallo), a Senegalese rap star whose Art Works for Change-supported Education sans Excision tour uses rap music to educate the West African public about the damage done to victims of female genital cutting (FGC) and gender-based violence. Fatou—who was herself a victim of FGC and rape—is not content, rarely seems happy, and on many days is not what the world might call "nice." And therein lies a large part of her power.

When I spend ten days touring with Fatou and her band throughout Senegal and The Gambia, she comports herself in much the same way that she raps, with staccato bursts of energy and an often impatient backbeat. She heads into regions where conservative Muslim groups have threatened her life because of her anti-FGC stance and wonders why others would hesitate to do the same. She eats rarely and little, sleeps minimally, and seems unaffected by the eighteen-hour days and 110-degree heat, impatiently reminding the less hearty in her entourage that they, too, must be stoic in the name of activism.

At an antiviolence event at a middle school in the Kolda region of Senegal, I watch with a sort of shocked awe as she leaves the dais, walks up to the respected United Nations speaker addressing the crowd, and whispers in her ear: "Be quick! You've been up here too long, and you are merely saying the same thing over and over." It may have been rudeness, or it may have been righteousness, but whatever it was, it worked: the speaker concluded her remarks, leaving time for a local woman to share her own story of FGC, rape, and forced marriage—testimony that would prove to be the most moving point in the day's program.

The political is as personal as it can possibly be for Fatou. Her lived experience with FGC, a practice that it is estimated over ninety-two million girls and women have undergone in Africa, informs all that she does. Brutal, painful and almost always performed without anesthesia, the generations-old practice of FGC was banned by the Senegalese Parliament in 1999. Yet what national law has rejected is often embraced or at least tolerated according to local customs, generating conflict within communities and families.

Fatou, who was cut at the age of three in a public ceremony, still remembers, vividly, that day. "I was with about fifty other girls in my village, and we were told this was a great celebration. We were laughing, dancing, playing—so free. This was the last time I ever again felt such freedom and trust. We were then taken into a room, one by one, where each of us was cut without anesthesia. I remember the blood and the pain even today. And I remember the feeling that my community had betrayed me. But mostly I remember feeling the betrayal of my mother. How could she allow this pain to come to me, her daughter whom I know she loved?"

"Over time, I came to understand that my mother was not cutting me to harm me, but because she felt that she was doing what was the best for me so that I could have a good future and could get married. The girl who is not cut is treated like an animal—she can't get married, cook, or even give water to someone. She is too 'unclean.' My mother was weak, too much believing in tradition, to stop this from happening to me. It was easier once I understood this about her, but not so easy that the pain ever went away. I knew that one day I must speak out about this. And when I found music and began to have success as a singer, I did talk out. I am lucky that my creativity and my music have given me a voice. So many other Senegalese women will never have that, so I use this voice for them."

Cutting is not the only form of gender-based violence Fatou has endured. At the age of six, she was sexually assaulted by a family member, an event that she almost never speaks of, but one that informs her antiviolence work in important ways. "So many of us African women who have been cut are also victims of other forms of sexual violence or abuse. I believe that those who do not understand what is wrong about cutting a girl may also be afraid to stand up against rape or incest if they are told that this is just all a part of 'how things are' for us. The mothers must be our first protectors. It is the mothers who must speak out about this, but it is the mothers who have themselves been harmed who are too silent, and we learn to be silent from them."

"I am not a total woman now," says Fatou. "I feel, how would you say, 'incomplete' in my body. I am angry that this cutting, this rape, this violence continues. Just weeks ago, I learned that they cut a girl in my own distant family. She was not yet one year old! People think that the national laws will solve the problem. But it is only the beginning of solving the problem if our mothers in the villages do not stand up in protection of their daughters. And we must educate those daughters to their rights, so that they know that they can also stand up for themselves."

"Sister Fa has been among the most powerful voices saying 'no' to FGC and violence against women in West Africa," says Fatou D. Niang, a respected women's rights advocate at the United Nations Educational, Scientific and Cultural Organization office in Senegal. "She succeeded as a musical artist here, and then in Europe. She could have turned her back on Senegal years ago, never coming home because of her success in rap in other countries. But she continues the fight here, and the young people and also older people are listening to her. They come out to hear the music and then they hear her message that FGC is against the law. But she also tells them that if they don't stand up for that law in their villages, the law will not matter. Someday this violence against our Senegalese girls will end. When it does, Sister Fa and her rap music will have played the largest possible role."

The rap scene in Senegal is active musically and politically—many of its musicians have strong ties to local human rights groups and United Nations nongovernmental organizations, and Fatou and her all-male band are at the forefront of that community. Her music is a sort of fusion-rap that marries soul, hip-hop, dance, and just a hint of reggae. Her lyrics address race, class, poverty, and female empowerment (and they still make you want to dance). Through the sheer force of her star power, her music, and her defining impatience, Fatou has encouraged a countrywide conversation about violence against women.

"Hip-hop, rap, they are supposed to be about protest," says Fatou. "That's the history of the music. I'm a rapper, but when you ask me how I define myself, I have to say that I am a human rights activist first. Rap music is a tool; it is how I put my beliefs into action. It can bring people together, tell a message of change. But only if we bring that music where it is needed. When others are afraid to go to communities where the anti-FGC message is not welcome, I do sometimes become angry at their fear. I tell my band that we must think of pain that girls in Senegal are enduring. Who are we to hesitate?"

Anger—a dread word for so many women I know—is something that Fatou has clearly embraced. The absence of contentment is not a deficit in her character, it is the defining aspect of her character. Though she is not always "nice," she is inarguably and deeply good. When I watch her performing an anti-FGC song in front of hundreds of screaming fans in the Casamance region during one of our final nights in Senegal, there are moments when she seems to literally shimmer with righteous indignation.

There is something exhilarating about time spent with Fatou. Sparks fly, the ineffectual or uncommitted scurry, and all of that magnificent friction leads to change. Bearing witness to it isn't always pleasant. But it is a privilege.

Grey Matters: **Christa Desir**

Christa Desir does not "do" guile. She has never been very good at crafting a story—about herself, or someone else—and editing out the parts that are complicated or messy. She is too honest, and too impatient, for that. She speaks first, thinks later, and finds that usually—though not always—that's OK. "I'm going to use a few 'f-bombs,'" she announces, as she rises to speak to an audience of Northwestern University students. "Are you cool with that?" (They are.)

It is tempting to describe Christa as a woman who has embraced contradiction. She's a lover of Converse Chuck Taylors who manages to look sweetly earnest in a headband, a pretty girl whose favorite song is Ani DiFranco's "Not a Pretty Girl," and a Sunday school teacher whose go-to T-shirt reads "I Write Banned Books." The truth is that these seemingly contradictory ideas are not necessarily contradictory at all. "Life is not black and white," Christa says. "Real people are messy and inconsistent, which is what makes them so great."

In her life and in her work as a young-adult novelist, the messy areas are what compel Christa. Her debut young-adult novel, *Fault Line*, is all about ambiguities. Christa wrote it from the perspective of a teenage boy, Ben, whose girlfriend Ani is raped at a high school party that he decides not to go to. Christa makes clear that a rape occurs—by any legal or moral standard, she leaves no doubt about that. But there is drinking. There is table dancing. There is texting. And there are high school kids—far too many for comfort—who fail to see what happens to Ani as rape at all. "I didn't write a feel-good, everything-is-gonna-be-all-right book about rape," Christa says. "I wish I could have, but that's not my book."

Fault Line is informed by, but not based on, Christa's own experience with sexual violence. She was five years old when she was separated from her family at a local shopping mall, and molested by a man who found her in the mall parking lot and offered to help her if she got in his car.

When the man dropped Christa off at the entrance to the mall about forty-five minutes later, she was a very different child. She was reunited with her father and sister almost as soon as she walked in the mall's front entrance—they had been desperately searching for her as soon as they realized that she had wandered off. Most of what Christa remembers about that reunion is "a lot of crying." Few questions were asked about what might have happened or where she had been for close to an hour. "I think everyone wanted to think, and probably really did think, that I had just wandered around lost, and then found my dad again."

Christa believes her childhood silence about being sexually assaulted was the product of what she calls an "almost instinctive" sense of responsibility for what had happened to her. "Even at five years old, I completely blamed myself for the fact that I had been sexually molested," Christa says. "I was the one who wandered away. I was the one who got in that man's car."

Years later, as Christa reflected on this, it reinforced her belief that the world starts sending messages to girls, almost from infancy, that they are responsible for their own safety and to blame when things go wrong: *Cross your legs. Don't run into the living room naked when company is here. You can't go outside until you put on a shirt (but your brother can).*

Christa remained silent about the violence she had lived through for over a decade. She says that during that time, she was only vaguely conscious of what had happened to her. A few years after she was assaulted, she recalls a halfhearted attempt to tell her sister about it— one in which she downplayed the abuse and obscured its details. "We were both young and clueless—so that pretty much went nowhere." Mostly Christa says that she "eliminated" it from her mind.

Christa was at a high school sleepover when one of her best girlfriends began to share—haltingly at first, and then with the confidence that comes from being listened to by sympathetic teenage girlfriends—that she had been molested by a family member. Christa's memories of her own experience with violence came back to her in that moment. "Not all of it," Christa says. "The details took a while to trickle out, but the basics were there." So that night Christa also spoke, for the first time, about having been sexually abused.

Hearing her own words made the violence feel real. It was a turning point—the moment when Christa realized that the more she shared her story with other survivors, the more "not alone" she felt. "That's the good part," says Christa. "The shitty part is that so many of us have some version of that story to tell."

As many survivors of childhood sexual violence do, Christa struggled during her teens. She wrestled with an eating disorder. She was a cutter. She made what those around her called "poor choices." From the distance of adulthood, Christa is able to understand that teenage self and feel a sort of gratitude to her. "Those shitty choices I made in my teens? They're part of what brought me into the woman I am, someone who loves and fights in equal measure."

In college, Christa became an activist on the issue of gender-based violence. "I'd rally. I'd drumbeat. Whatever it took, I was there—because it was so awesome to be connected to other women who had gone through this." Christa has remained involved in the anti-rape movement ever since. She says that her volunteer work as an emergency room advocate wasn't so much eye-opening as affirming of the disconnect between what the media tells us about rape and what it looks like close up.

"When you are sitting in the hospital, holding the hand of a high school girl whose life has just been torn apart by rape, it is very real and raw and awful," Christa says. "It doesn't look like it does in the victim-blaming outside world."

Christa has been a reader since she was a little girl: "*Bastard Out of Carolina*; *Girl, Interrupted*; *Speak*; even *Forever* by Judy Blume." She has also always loved writing. After college, and a series of day jobs organized around no specific theme—"my husband Julio says that he and my activism have been the only constant in my adult life"— Christa settled into book editing and began to explore the idea of writing a young-adult novel of her own.

Taking part in The Stories We Tell, the Voices and Faces Project's testimonial writing workshop for survivors, a program created by novelist R. Clifton Spargo, was a step in that direction. Christa calls the experience of taking part in an intensive, two-day writing workshop "life-changing."

"It wasn't just about writing during those two days," Christa says. "It was about reading, listening, and understanding that what we write about rape isn't just about us—it's about hearing the stories of other women and having the courage to weave their experiences into our work. It's about telling the hard stories that people don't always want to hear."

During the workshop, Christa became especially close to Sarah Sullivan, a fellow writer. Sarah and three of her friends had been hiking the Appalachian Trail when they were gang-raped by a group of local men. Subsequently, the four girls were shamed by the police, blamed by the media—their names were published in the local paper in order to "discourage false reporting"—and largely unsupported by their families. Before they were raped, Sarah told the group that she and her three friends had been "pretty normal, slightly screwed-up teenagers who drank and smoked pot." After the trial and the subsequent media exposure, they were "hanging by a thread."

"Sarah is just this beautiful person and writer, and her story just rocked that room," Christa recalls. "She told us that she and two of the girls were able to move on after this happened—it took a lot of work, there was a lot of struggle, but they did it. But that the fourth girl, Sarah's friend Rita, never got over it, and spiraled down into drugs, became homeless, and more or less disappeared. I remember Sarah's exact words about Rita that day, and how much pain was contained in those words: 'We lost her.'"

During an overnight exercise, workshop participants were asked to write about rape from the point of view of someone of a different gender or sexual orientation. That night, Christa began to explore a new story, about a seventeen-year-old boy trying, and failing, to save the girlfriend he loves as she struggles to rebuild her life after a gang rape. During the second day of the workshop, Christa shared the beginnings of that story. She says that the responses in that room— "from the writers, from Clifton, even my own internal response as I read it out loud—it just felt very right"—told Christa that she was onto something.

Christa began to write her novel. "When you go on a spa vacation with your mom and sisters, and you don't even want to leave your hotel room because you are so into your story—that's a pretty good sign," Christa says. Six months later, Christa sold her "dark, truthful little book about rape," *Fault Line*, to Simon and Schuster.

"That my book found a home was kind of shocking to me," Christa says. "And yet . . . not. Because I believed that this story needed to be out there in the world. And there were other people— not a lot of them, but enough of them—who believed in it, too."

"*Fault Line* is not my story, and it's not Sarah's story," Christa says. "It was inspired by more women than I can ever recognize, inspired by every rape victim I have ever listened to or read about whose story has broken my heart. This book is for them."

Christa's book was inspired by something else: her belief that good boys and men are the "missing piece" in the fight to end sexual violence. Writing a young-adult novel about rape in which a teenage boy is a "kind of" hero, instead of the inevitable villain, was important to Christa.

"When I talk about *Fault Line* and the issue of sexual violence at a high school or on a college campus I always, always open by telling the audience that I am very 'pro-dude,'" Christa says. "If we keep telling boys that they are always the problem, how can we expect them to see themselves as part of any sort of solution?"

Christa believes that gender politics are a complicated thing. "I'd love for this to be a world where teenage girls are so confident that they don't care what the cute guy thinks, or so self-respecting that it doesn't matter if the boys respect them back," Christa says. "You know what? That's not our world—not for most teenage girls, anyway. So we've got to reach the boys if we want to change anything."

At the center of Christa's own life are three boys—her husband, Julio, and her two sons—and her "gorgeous, sensitive" daughter (with whom she is photographed). There's also a "kind of crazy" dog who is Christa's constant writing companion. Christa's says that her family is her rock. "Where am I happiest? Always, always with Julio and my kids.

"I got lucky with Julio—he is my centerline, the tether that keeps me from floating away," Christa says. "He is so proud of this book.

He worries about losing me to flashbacks about rape, yet if I wanted to give up my writing and editing to be a full-time activist on sexual violence, I know he'd say, 'OK, I got you.'"

I ask Christa how she identifies herself first—as a writer or an activist. "Activist, always," Christa says. "Because I may not write for the rest of my life. But I will be fighting to end rape until the day I die."

The need for that fight was made real to Christa when she read some of the online comments posted about *Fault Line* ("I know—totally idiotic to do that. But I couldn't stop myself."). People either love her book or hate it—not a bad place to be for a writer—and the haters often bemoan the lack of a happy ending, wish Ani were a less complicated young woman, or wonder why Ben can't be a better hero ("It's *so* not *Twilight*"). And then they debate, endlessly, whether what happened to Ani was rape.

"I wrote a book with deeply human characters and gray areas," Christa says. "The one thing that I never treated as gray was the idea that a rape occurred. You know, I actually expected kids to have discussions about that—if Steubenville has taught me anything, it's that a lot of teenage kids don't 'get' what rape is, and want to downplay or ignore it. And I wanted to acknowledge that and start a dialogue that their parents and teachers could help drive—because talking is the beginning of changing things when it comes to teens.

"But when adults read *Fault Line* and post things like 'I don't have a lot of sympathy for drunk girls who cry rape,' where do you go with that?" Christa asks. "Because a comment like that isn't about my book or my characters; it's about a way too many people and too many parents see the issue of rape. How do you feel positive when 'grownups' are still saying stuff like this in 2013?"

Christa the realist says this, barely pauses—she is not much of a pauser—and then shifts into Christa the optimist. "But their kids are still open," she says. "That's the awesome thing about a teenage mind: it can be shaped. It can even be changed. It's way too soon to give up on them."

From left to right: Edith Rosales Gutierrez, Norma Jimenez Osorio, Italia Mendez Moreno, and Claudia Hernandez Martinez

Freedom in Motion:
The Women of Atenco, Mexico

Italia Mendez Moreno knew that she was, at last, going to lose consciousness, which frightened her even more than the thought of remaining awake and aware of all that was being done to her. Over the
course of the previous few hours, she had been taken from a private
home, brutally beaten, thrown into a police bus on top of dozens of
other battered and broken bodies, and then raped. Now she was in a
lineup of women who were ordered to press their foreheads against
the seats of the bus, their backsides vulnerable to further violation. It
was then that the consciousness she had clung to for hours began to
ooze out of her.

"But I began to hear a voice, and the person pressed next to me
was saying, 'Look at me.' I did, and for the first time I saw Norma,"
says Italia three years later, as she recounts the violence she endured
on May 4, 2006. "She began talking to me very calmly, until I could
focus again and feel my body again, and that kept me from fainting.
It was like love at first sight. Later, when another woman in the bus
became hysterical, I was able to calm her because of what Norma had
taught me."

"I did not know Norma before, and now I cannot imagine my life
without her," continues Italia. "She is my sister." As she turns toward
Norma Jimenez Osorio, who is seated next to her, Italia's eyes—which
are large and dark and had until that point remained unsmiling—lose
their somber look and seem almost joyful. Italia's memory of being
calmed by Norma in the past moves her in the present.

Italia, Norma, Claudia Hernandez Martinez, and Edith Rosales
Gutierrez are sharing their stories with me in a spartan but bright

room at Center Prodh, a Jesuit-founded human rights organization based in Mexico City. The center has engaged in a seven-year legal battle on behalf of these four women and seven others who were raped and tortured by the Mexican police during a May 2006 raid in San Salvador Atenco. The story of the Women of Atenco—as they are known to the international human rights community—is a window into a country where state-sanctioned rape and sexual torture are used to repress activist communities, squelch civil unrest, and marginalize Latinas.

San Salvador Atenco, a municipality of the state of Mexico, has been the scene of populist protest and government ire since 2002, when local farmers successfully halted government plans to build a national airport on their land. Four years later, on May 3, 2006, a group of flower sellers who had negotiated a labor agreement that was to have allowed them to set up stalls in a nearby downtown area arrived at the market square and found police waiting for them. In the ensuing protest, which would last for two days, dozens were seriously injured, and two people—including a fourteen-year-old boy—were killed.

On May 4, the protests continued in Atenco, drawing aid groups, human rights activists, investigative journalists, and volunteers seeking to help the wounded. Among those arriving that morning were Edith, who was participating in a health brigade organized by her labor union; Italia, who worked for a foundation focused on at-risk children; Norma, who wanted to write about the protests for a feminist magazine; and Claudia, who was a political science student at the time of the protests. None of them had been on the ground in Atenco long before local, state, and federal police began to use beatings, house raids, and indiscriminate detentions to take control of the city. Of the hundreds detained during the police crackdown, forty-seven were women.

Edith, who was fifty-one years old at the time of the protests, remembers May 4 well. She was preparing to care for the injured when the police first fired tear gas in her direction. She began to run and was swiftly apprehended by several officers. "I feel they are pulling on my hair, pulling me backward, beating me all over my body, and then they make a row and begin to kick me down. I try to raise my hands to keep from falling, and they beat me with their nightsticks . . . saying 'Get up, whore.' Later they throw me in a bus where people were piled on top of each other, and I hear them say, 'We are going to stick them from behind.'"

Edith was raped, beaten, and sexually assaulted during the hours-long ride to an area prison, and beaten again upon arrival. Ultimately, more than two dozen women reported that they had also been raped, sexually assaulted, beaten, or tortured on the ground in Atenco, in the police bus, or at the area prison where the detainees were held.

After local authorities publicly dismissed their calls for justice, the women of Atenco initially turned to the federal attorney general's office with their case. After two years of being denied justice at both the state and local levels, they took their case to the Inter-American Commission on Human Rights, with the legal support of Center Prodh and the Center for Justice and International Law. In 2009, the Mexican Supreme Court issued a statement affirming that there were widespread human rights abuses at the hands of police and urging the prosecution of those responsible. Yet, though dozens of police officers were identified by prosecutors as presumed perpetrators of the violence against these women, only three people have been tried. One was given a sentence of time served, and a small fine, which was overturned on appeal. Two cases are ongoing. Ranking officers and political authorities at the highest levels of government—those ulti-mately responsible for the human rights violations on their watch—remain untouched.

"What happened in Atenco is not an isolated case," says Stepha-nie Erin Brewer, a Center Prodh attorney who has represented the eleven women before the Inter-American Commission. "This is a high-profile example of a broader use of repression and torture—in particular, sexual torture as a weapon against women—to try to crush social protest. What is extraordinary about this case is the ceaseless struggle of these women."

"These survivors were willing to do what the government never imagined they would do: say to the world, 'Yes, I was raped by the Mexican police.' And they have continued to do this despite the free-dom of the police who did this to them and the power of the authori-ties implicated in their case."

The women of Atenco are pushing back against that power with a weapon of their own: their voices. With the support of Amnesty International and other human rights groups, they have shared their stories in the United States and Europe, with representatives from the European Union, and with other foreign governments, and they have been joined in their fight by activists and organizations from dozens of countries. Their case remains a high priority for Amnesty, which is driving a multi-year letter-writing campaign on their behalf, and for Centro Prodh, where lawyers continue to fight on behalf of the women.

In 2009 and 2012, Claudia traveled to Chicago on behalf of Women of Atenco, calling for the end of impunity for all who commit rape and torture. The case resonated deeply in a city with its own history of police brutality, which is most often unleashed against women and men of color. "I was surprised by how many people in Chicago supported us," says Claudia. "Some said to me that they had gone through similar situations with the police in the United States. We gave strength to them as we spoke of our case, and they gave strength to us with their stories. This is not only a problem in Mexico; it is something systemic on a larger scale."

Given the freedom of the men who did this to them, and the power of the politicians who have been accused of either tacitly or actively encouraging such violence, I ask Italia, Norma, Edith, and Claudia if they have ever hesitated in their pursuit of justice. Their answers are varied, but the CliffsNotes version of each is a resounding "no."

"If something should [happen to us], people would know about it because we accuse our assailants," says Claudia, leaning forward. "We denounce what the government is doing and the individuals who did it. We denounce those involved in the case, such as Enrique Pena Nieto (now President of Mexico) and Eduardo Medina-Mora (now Mexican ambassador to the United States). We say it clearly: it is they who were responsible for sexual abuse, kidnapping, and murders."

"Once someone asked me if I was scared when I was arrested," says Edith. "I was scared, but then I thought, 'Now, it's my turn.' We are not the first ones; it has happened to other women who protest, and also to everyday people who were at home in their beds when the police broke in. Yet, of course, it is hard to believe it when you yourself have to live through it."

That simple statement—"Now it's my turn"—underscores something I find especially compelling about these women. During the time that I spend with them, they seem utterly without self-pity, even when pity of one's self would be understandable (and perhaps even psychologically beneficial). The women of Atenco rarely speak of the violence that they lived through as a personal, or even a collective, tragedy. Instead, they talk about it as a political event. They look backward at the stories of their mothers and grandmothers and generations of Latina women who have been victims of sexual violence. They look forward, imagining the new world that they are working to create, one in which those who rape and torture will never do so with impunity. But they do not seem to often look inward. These are women who prefer the word "we" to the word "I."

Yet something shifts in the room when we begin to talk about those whose stories are at once ever present and rarely told: the women who survived sexual violence and torture in Atenco physically but never returned from it psychologically. "Some of us had more to rebuild our lives with than others," says Edith. "Many of our companions didn't have access to help. They were released from jail later than we were, they moved, and they didn't have access (to our community). Their escape was to withdraw. Not all of us experienced the same conditions in terms of economics or family support."

Italia nods, adding that that disparity in resources and experiences among the over two dozen women who were victims haunts her in a way that is difficult to explain. "This caused me more pain and stress than the actual torture. It was a strange feeling, between guilt and something else, knowing that some of my companions didn't receive therapy or were in jail longer than I was."

It is then that Claudia leans forward to speak. She is physically small, but from the moment I first met her, she radiated fearlessness with her willingness to "name names" and her tendency to speak rapidly while gesturing sharply with her hands. Nothing about her could be described as soft. But now she begins to speak slowly, as if she is uncertain that she wants to move forward. But she does.

"When I got out of jail, I stayed in my house for a year," says Claudia. "I cried, and I suffered so much. I had had plans for the future with my partner, but when I got out of jail, he left me. I felt like the whole world had turned its back on me because I was a rape victim. During that time, I began to drink a lot, and I started to go to a lot of bars. I did many things I didn't normally do. And then I realized that the government had tied me up for a moment. They laid the first stone of my destruction. But even with all of this, I said to myself, 'I am still Claudia! I am still Claudia! I was raped, but this does not take away my dignity.'"

Earlier in the day, Norma, who is the quietest of the women, described the first time she saw the faces of the other women who had been raped and tortured during the raid on Atenco: "When we were first in prison, they separated the women from the men and made us look down. When I could finally lift up my face, and I see all my companions who I had never met before, I recognized myself in them."

I recognized myself in them. Norma's words were the most gorgeous (albeit unconscious) definition of sisterhood I had ever heard, and Claudia's testimony is an expression of that same idea. By all appearances, Claudia has gone on with her life and used her experience with violence to give that life a new purpose. She might have merely sympathized with those who were unable to do something similar. But instead she identified with them, seeing herself and the most painful pieces of her story in their struggle.

Claudia's words connected her experience to the experiences of almost every rape survivor I have ever interviewed. There is violence, there is grief, and there is the expression of that grief, which can take many and often painful forms (turning to alcohol being one of the most common). Then there is the realization that, underneath all of our sadness and self-harm, we are still there, facing the challenge of coming to terms with who we once were and who we now are.

It has been over seven years since the events in Atenco, and today the case exists in a legal limbo. The federal government has claimed that, because the perpetrators are state police, they must be prosecuted in Mexico State. The state government, aware that the Inter-American Commission is analyzing the case, has opened criminal trials of just two of the dozens of named perpetrators but has not officially accepted jurisdiction over their cases. The remaining police and other authorities responsible for the violence against the women of Atenco roam free in a country where rape and sexual abuse have

reached epidemic levels. Over 120,000 rapes—one every four minutes—occur in Mexico each year. A 2012 report co-produced by the
Nobel Women's Initiative and Just Associates found that government
officials and their security forces were often the worst perpetrators of
sexualized violence used to "intimidate and subdue" women.

"This is an ongoing struggle," says Stephanie Erin Brewer, "because the Mexican government can see that they cannot outlast or ex-
haust these women. This case is not going to disappear. The women
of Atenco and their allies are not only in this fight for the long run;
they are in it for life." As they await the Inter-American Commission's ruling on their case, the women of Atenco have launched Freedom in Motion, a new campaign against impunity. The campaign is
both a reminder to the government that the Atenco women are not
resting until they have justice and a clarion call to the community:
Get engaged. Get involved. Change things.

When I ask the women what justice will look like, Edith again
turns her attention to the broader struggle. "It is not enough for the
perpetrators to pay for what they have done to us as individuals. Justice will arrive only when there is change for the benefit of all people."

Claudia nods, but qualifies her agreement. "Yes, justice will be
something systemic, a social change. But it will be a very long transformation that perhaps we will not live to see."

The Voice: **Jennifer Hopper**

I expected her to be someone else.

I had been introduced to Jennifer Hopper—or rather, the idea of Jennifer Hopper—through a long and emotional e-mail that I received from a former colleague, Jean Fox. Jean, who is typically neither long-winded nor emotional, was writing me just weeks after the rape and murder of her closest friend, Teresa Butz. Jennifer had been Teresa's partner, and she had also been raped and stabbed, but survived the attack.

Jean knew of my own history of violence, and it was clear that she wanted to reach out to someone who might understand her grief over the loss of her best friend. It also seemed clear that she had a desire to connect me to Jennifer. The details in Jean's e-mail painted a grim and very sad picture: *they were planning to marry in the fall . . . home invasion . . . raped repeatedly . . . begged for their lives . . . Teresa died saving Jen.* "How can Jennifer Hopper ever come back from living through and witnessing this violence," I remember thinking. "How can she even get out of bed every day?"

And yet here is Jennifer, standing up and extending her hand as I enter the restaurant where Jean has arranged for the three of us to meet, almost a year to the day after she and Teresa were attacked. Nothing about Jennifer's affect seems fragile. She is dark-haired and very pretty—the kind of pretty that refuses to blend into a crowd—and she is wearing a blouse that doesn't hide the four slash-shaped scars on her neck. It's not that she needs you to see them. It's just that she has no intention of spending the rest of her life hiding them.

Both Jennifer's handshake and the spontaneous hug it evolves into are firm. This is not the hug of someone hanging on. It's the hug of a woman saying, "I am here." During our first, long dinner together, I discover that being present is one of Jennifer's most distinctive qualities. She looks you in the eye and doesn't let go, especially as she shares the most painful details from that night. She does not lower her voice when she says the word "rape." She tells me that this has not always been the case, that what she lived through has made her less worried about making others uncomfortable. But when she says this, she will swallow and pause, because the price that has been paid for her willingness to speak candidly has been far too great.

Teresa Butz was a Seattle property manager and Jennifer a Boston Conservatory–trained singer working in communications when they were introduced by a mutual friend. "I think I started to fall in love with Teresa the moment I met her," Jennifer tells me. "People say, 'Oh, that person loved life,' but Teresa really, really loved life. She had this way with people that probably came from growing up with so many brothers and sisters—she was just funny and crazy and incredibly alive.

"But she had a giving side, too—she was really compassionate," Jennifer continues. "She was on the board of the Compass Housing Alliance (a Seattle homeless shelter), and she was so into that. She rarely passed a homeless person on the street without giving money or asking them if they were OK. She just had that kind of awesome heart."

Jennifer pauses, laughs suddenly, and says, "All right, I have to stop myself here. Just so you know, Teresa was not a saint. There was the drinking, and she couldn't quite give up smoking, and we both loved to eat way, way too much. But her flaws just made her so awesomely human."

They moved into a small house in Seattle's South Park neighborhood, a diverse enclave where the homes were still affordable. In the summer of 2009, they began planning a commitment ceremony for that fall. "We were at that stage where you start to talk about everything that makes up your history, the obscure details about each other, 'I lived on that street when I was twelve, in high school this was what I was like, let me tell you this story about me and my brother.' We were just talking and talking that whole summer, about our pasts and also about the kind of future we wanted together. One of the things we were talking about was having children together; it was actually one of the last conversations we had."

As I listen to Jennifer, I find myself thinking about memory. Can we ever recall the days before a trauma without their taking on a nostalgic glow? However mundane, however full of everyday stresses or ordinary pleasures, the past becomes beautiful in retrospect because we lived it as innocents not yet initiated into the world's cruelties. But nostalgia isn't always false, and it seems clear to me that those last few months of Jennifer and Teresa's life together were genuinely blissful ones. They were in love enough to be sure of their future but also new enough to say the things that, over time, couples often fail or forget to say.

"I said 'I love you' to Teresa that last night, before we fell asleep, and I am so, so grateful not to have left that unsaid," Jennifer says. Yet that comforting memory doesn't mitigate Jennifer's grief. If anything, all that hope and love, robbed so suddenly of its object, seems to have been both a gift and a burden for her. The "might-have-beens" in Jennifer's life are as lovely as they are cruel.

The night that she and Teresa were attacked is precisely etched in Jennifer's memory, even as it felt, at first, like a dream. "I woke up suddenly, and there was a naked man holding a knife to my neck. The terror I felt was so strong that I kind of went out of my body; it was like I was looking down and watching this man standing over us, thinking, no, this only happens in nightmares or films. But as soon as he spoke— he said, 'Shut up, I won't hurt you, I just want pussy'—I thought, 'Oh, my God, this is real.'"

Isaiah Kalebu had a long history of unstable and violent behavior. In the sixteen months prior to the attack, he had been in and out of the mental health and judicial systems, had threatened to kill his own mother, and had a restraining order taken out on him by his aunt. A state psychologist advised King County Superior Court that Kalebu represented "an elevated risk for future danger to others and for committing future criminal acts," advising that he be held in a mental health facility. But six days before he entered Jennifer and Teresa's home, a superior court judge allowed Kalebu to go free. The use he made of that freedom was devastating.

Over the course of the next ninety minutes, Kalebu, who was armed with two knives, raped Jennifer and Teresa multiple times, in multiple ways. "Each of us feared that if we fought back or did anything, he would use the knife on the other. In that room, time sort of stopped. I was afraid that if I even spoke to Teresa, or tried to touch her to comfort her, he would hurt us. It was the most horrific thing to not be able to reach out when we so needed each other.

"One of the worst moments was when I looked in Teresa's eyes, and I felt like I saw her dying before he had even used that knife on her, before she had died," says Jennifer. "It's hard to explain this, but being raped like that, her seeing me raped like that . . . it just killed her spirit before it killed her body."

That psychic pain did not stand in the way of Teresa engaging in a final fight for their lives. "He had us pressed down on the bed, using his knees to hold each of us down, and when he began to stab us, we tried to use our hands for protection. I heard Teresa say 'you got me' and my mind just screamed 'no, no, no!' But he had also slashed my neck, and I began to bleed so much that I just thought, 'this is it'— and I remember thinking that I hoped what Teresa believed about heaven was true. And then suddenly I felt this huge surge of energy inside me."

It was Teresa who, despite having been stabbed in the heart, resisted Kalebu with a final and almost supernatural show of strength, kicking him off the bed, and grabbing a bedside table to fight him off. It's an effort that Jennifer believes saved her life.

The events of the rest of that night—Kalebu fleeing, Jennifer running naked and bleeding into the street, a teenage neighbor (the first person to respond to Jennifer's cries) removing her own clothes to try to stop Teresa's bleeding—blur. As police and paramedics converged on the scene, a barely conscious Teresa begged those who were treating her to tell her mother that she loved her, and then said her final words: "He told us if we did what he asked us to do, he wouldn't hurt us. He lied. He lied."

And Jennifer, who was close enough to see but not touch Teresa, screamed out words of her own: "Fight, Teresa, fight. I love you."

But Jennifer says that she already knew in her heart that it was too late. "Still, I kept asking, 'Is she OK, Is she OK?'" No one would answer her. Finally, at the hospital, Jennifer learned that Teresa had died outside their home. And then her last hope, that she and Teresa would be able to get through this together—"that door, it just closed."

One of the most striking things about living through violence is the contrast between the isolation felt by victims during a crime—in Jennifer's words, "we were so alone in that house, the most alone I've ever felt"—and the constant activity that descends on survivors once the machinery of justice is set in motion. For Jennifer, released from the hospital with stitches on her neck and arm, this meant giving a statement to the police and working with a forensic artist to develop a sketch of the perpetrator (thanks in part to Jennifer's description, Kalebu was caught and charged with rape and murder just days after the attack). It also meant finding a new place to live, because the home she had shared with Teresa was now officially a crime scene.

Jennifer watched her own story play out in the media. The case led the Seattle nightly news for a week and made national headlines. Seeing photos of Teresa on the TV screen, and hearing herself referred to as "Butz's partner" was both painful and merciful. "It was so weird to watch the news and know that the anonymous person they were talking about was me. But that privacy the media allowed me was a protective bubble, and that bubble allowed me to grieve in private, which I so needed."

Comfort came in the form of Jennifer's mother, stepfather, and grandmother, Teresa's large and loving family, and a community of friends and supporters that Jennifer calls "her angels." Two of those angels were Jean Fox and Rachel Ebeling, Teresa's best friends since childhood.

Rachel, Jean, and Teresa had a close, thirty-five-year relationship that never wavered, continuing from early childhood through high school, college, marriages, children, and life on two different continents. "It was like the three of us were having this lifelong conversation," says Jean. "And it was the best kind of conversation, one where a mutual language of understanding had been developed because we had known and loved each other for as long as we could remember. When we met Jennifer, we fell in love with her, too."

It was Jean's idea to produce a benefit album to honor Teresa, one that would feature performances by Jennifer and the extended Butz family. The Butzes are extraordinarily musical—Teresa's brother, Norbert Butz, Jr., is a Grammy- and Tony-winning Broadway star, and three generations of the clan write and perform songs. At Teresa's funeral service in her hometown of St. Louis, music became their method for articulating the pain that they were feeling and, for a few merciful moments, transcending that pain.

Teresa's philosophy, according to Jean, could be summed up in three statements: *Let's do it. Why wait? Go!* "So I felt like I was sort of channeling Teresa when I had the idea to do a tribute album, because I had absolutely no clue what it would take to produce a CD. But, hey, why let that stop me?" Jean says with a laugh. Jennifer takes the channeling idea a bit more seriously. "I actually think that Jean *was* channeling Teresa," she says. "Only Teresa could have understood how much I needed something like this to get me out of myself. Some people come to you after a loss and bring a casserole. Jean and Rachel brought the idea of a benefit album. But what they really did was invite me into their world to heal."

Jennifer and the Butz family decided early on that the CD should benefit victims of rape. "We all felt that there were people who didn't want to talk about that, they just wanted us to sort of leave the fact of the rapes out, especially when we talked about Teresa," says Jennifer. "But this wasn't just violence, it was sexual violence. I know that Teresa would have spoken out about that, and I wanted to speak out about it—because it was our truth."

They called the CD *Take You With Me*, after a song that Teresa's niece Hannah wrote and performed in her aunt's honor. Their newly formed band—made up of Jennifer, three generations of the Butz family, and a host of Norbert Butz's Broadway colleagues—was called the Angel Band. Featuring tracks written and performed by various Butz family members, and songs written by the likes of Bob Dylan and Mary Chapin Carpenter, *Take You With Me* was recorded in four cities where Teresa had family and friends who wanted to honor her memory. It has raised thousands of dollars for victims of sexual violence.

The recording sessions allowed those who loved Teresa best to remain closely connected as they tried to heal. Of course, the sessions were also a constant reminder that Teresa herself was no longer with them. "That first year without her was filled with disbelief and deep sadness," says Rachel Ebeling, who co-produced the album with Jean. "The Angel Band Project was our way of finding something good to cling to despite the tragic way that Teresa had died."

Her work with the Angel Band Project also provided a space for Jennifer to begin speaking out in a more public way. "At first I could talk about Teresa being murdered, but it was difficult for me to even say the word rape," says Jennifer. "What was awesome about coming together to make this record was that we were all finding our voices. Not our singing voices, our *voices* on the issue of sexual violence."

Jennifer's voice was equally resonant when she made the decision to testify at the 2011 trial of Isaiah Kalebu. A crime, when recounted in court testimony, is often a recitation of facts: *at this time, in this place, such and such was done to me.* But Jennifer's testimony transcended that form. Her words were like a eulogy for Teresa, a recounting of not only what had been done, but what had been lost. As she talked about Teresa and shared pieces of their history, Jennifer made the human cost of violence so real that few people in the courtroom could look away—and so heartbreaking that almost everyone wanted to.

"Those final days—not just the crime, but the good days before—are so etched in my memory, that they all just came pouring out during that trial," says Jennifer. "When I testified, I wanted them to really know who Teresa was as a person. I didn't want them to only know her as a crime victim. I told the jury about our last day together, how one of our friends got us to take a bus tour of microbreweries in the South Park area. During the bus ride, Teresa bartended, which of course was very Teresa. It was hot—she wouldn't think it was hot, she was from St. Louis, but trust me, it was hot—and she was sort of leaning back to catch the sun as it shown down on her, and when I glanced at her, I remember feeling so much love for her, and thinking, 'She is so happy today. This is the kind of day that she lived for.'"

But during Jennifer's six hours on the stand, she also shared the most painful and graphic details of that night. "It is the hardest thing in the world to do that, to talk about violence and sexual violence. It's not that I was ashamed. But it is not easy to say certain things in front of your family, your partner's family, people who know you but may not know that side of you, because why would they? Sometimes it would all just catch up with me—moments when they would show evidence from the crime scene in court, my own things that he touched being held up for everyone to view—and I would suddenly feel what had happened was real."

Journalist Eli Sanders, who won a Pulitzer Prize for his coverage of the Kalebu trial, called Jennifer "the bravest woman in Seattle." Juror JoAnn Wuitschick recalled in a post-trial interview that after the prosecution's graphic opening summary, she worried that she had overestimated her ability to wrap her mind around such a brutal crime. "I thought, 'Why am I here?'" All of that fell away when Jennifer took the stand. "Her directness, her composure, and her posture . . . it seemed she wanted not only to tell her story, but to tell Teresa's story," said Wuitschick. "I was honored to hear about how their relationship started, how it blossomed . . . what they were planning. I was so honored."

The jury found Kalebu guilty on multiple counts, and he was sentenced to life in prison without possibility of release. Jennifer and members of the Butz family, who had been there every day of the trial, spoke at the sentencing. They shared their deep sense of loss, they expressed their sadness, but they exhibited precious little bitterness. Teresa's brother Jim, studying to be a pastor, talked about the deep love that he had for his older sister, read from a bible that Teresa had given him, and told Kalebu that he hoped to see him in heaven. Teresa's father, Norbert, offered Kalebu his family's forgiveness, calling the man who had murdered his daughter by his first name—a detail that speaks to Teresa's parent's insistence on treating Kalebu with a dignity that he had never afforded their daughter. When Jennifer stood to speak, she talked about the horrors of that night, the depth of her loss, and her desire that Kalebu never be free to hurt anyone again. She then looked him in the eye and wished him peace.

In the years that have followed the sentencing, Jennifer has worked to reconstruct her life without the pillar that was Teresa. She's learning that it's OK to be sexual again. She's finding ways to honor Teresa's memory while remaining open to the possibility of a new love. And she's surrounding herself with people who are genuine—and who want her to be genuine, too. "Now I'll go to the party even if it's one of those days when I am on the verge of tears—because the people who really matter will want to take my truth."

Jennifer is not a believer in the concept of closure. After Kalebu's trial, she was asked whether the verdict had brought her peace.
"What I said then I feel even more strongly now: I'm grateful he was
put away. The world is safer, and I feel safer, but justice doesn't bring
peace. It only brings justice."

Still, time has helped. "I still feel lost without Teresa, but not sad
in the way I did for so long," says Jennifer. "I can hear a song that is
incredible, or feel the love of someone who has helped me heal, and
realize that yes, the world can still be glorious. Those two things, extreme grief and joy, can live in the same room. They have to for me."

Somehow through all of this, Jennifer continues to become *more*—
more thoughtful, more vital, and more purposeful. We sit down to
talk the morning after she performs a sold-out Angel Band Project
benefit concert in St. Louis, raising tens of thousands of dollars for
sexual violence survivors, and I tell her this. She smiles. "After all of
these years, I am starting to like my 'new' self better than the person I
was before. I am more intentional now. I am at my best when I speak
out about who I am, what I have been through, and what I want to
change. I have not let fear stop me from that. And I have loved learning what I am capable of."

Jennifer Hopper is such a force that it is tempting to resort to
easy affirmations when recounting her history. And yet Jennifer and
Teresa's story exists as a negation of every wrongheaded cliché about
survival that I have ever heard: *There's a reason for everything* (There
can be no good reason for rape and torture); *God wouldn't give you
anything you can't handle* (A merciful God would never give anyone
an experience like this); *What doesn't kill you only makes you stronger*
(What didn't kill Jennifer did kill Teresa, and it irrevocably alters the
lives of millions of sexual violence victims across the globe).

I ask Jennifer if there's one thing she wants the world to understand about sexual violence, and she doesn't hesitate for a moment.
"I want people to know that rape kills even if it doesn't kill," she
says. "Isaiah Kalebu killed the idea of me and Teresa the minute he
walked into our room that night. She was the love of my life, but I'm
not sure that we could have made it (as a couple) after what we went
through. She witnessed me being raped and suffering, and I saw her
go through the same, and more."

"That night changed us both," Jennifer says. "If she had lived, neither of us would have been the same person again, and I don't know that we could have had the same love again. There was so much between us, and that love I have for her is still right here in me. But could we have gotten through this? I don't know."

She says this fiercely, she says this sadly, and she says this because she is a woman willing to embrace one of the hardest truths of all: that even the strongest bonds can be crushed under the weight of awful events. Jennifer will never know if her relationship with Teresa could have survived Isaiah Kalebu. But it's clear she would give anything to have had the chance to try.

It's (Not) All About the Children

It has been said that you can get by in a country where you don't speak the local language with fifty oft-used words. Recently, I developed my own pet language theory: that being fluent in twenty-five globally recognized clichés will do almost as well.

I first meet Adama Mbengue, the national coordinator of the Forum for African Women Educationalists (FAWE), at the organization's offices in Dakar, Senegal. FAWE is working in thirty-two African countries, creating programs that address violence against women and girls, and fighting for their right to an education in a country where only 16 percent of girls go on to secondary school. Adama has been at the forefront of FAWE's efforts in Senegal, and she is extraordinary by any measure. I don't need to speak her primary language, which is French, to see that she commands respect wherever she goes. One of Adama's loveliest qualities is her warmth. When we are introduced and I extend my hand, she takes it in both of hers, pulls it close to her heart and says "Aah, Anna." I decide that I like her. I decide I need to change the pronunciation of my name. I want desperately to speak better French.

Adama and I will spend the next seven days traveling together, taking part in a tour to educate communities in southern Senegal about national policies on rape, incest, forced marriage, and female genital cutting. The broader delegation we are traveling with is large, and its two interpreters much in demand, so Adama and I are often left to our own conversational devices.

During the third day of the trip, as we sit in the back of the World Vision van that is ferrying us down a dusty, impossibly bumpy road in the southern Kolda region, Adama and I share a banana and attempt to talk about the girl-focused work we are doing in our respective countries. Adama knows about as much English as I do French, so there is a great deal of nodding and smiling of the "I think I understand you, but I'm not sure" variety. Then, as we near our destination—a school in a small rural village—I hear myself say, "Well, it's all about the children."

It's a phrase I don't remember ever using before—it must have sprung from the place where my mind stores its clichés and tropes. But upon hearing these words, Adama lights up. She nods vigorously. And then she repeats those words with an authority that tells me that they are familiar to her. I have made rhetorical contact.

Google "it's all about the children," and you'll get over two million results. It's one of those catchphrases that may once have been expressed as opinion, but is now widely accepted as fact. In most circles, saying that we do what we do for the next generation is as uncontroversial—and irrefutable—as asserting that blue sky, sunshine, and seventy-degree weather makes for a beautiful day.

Our tour of Senegal is a manifestation of this philosophy. We spend the lion's share of each day in the schools, and speaker after speaker has crafted her words with young people in mind. When Adama stands to speak, she addresses the girls directly. She tells them that they have the right to lives free of any form of violence or exploitation. She details the Senegalese laws that protect those rights. And she reminds the girls, to loud cheers and enthusiastic clapping, that it is their African mothers who fought long and hard for the protections that are now Senegalese law.

There is something gorgeous—this is the word that most naturally springs to mind—about watching these girls celebrate their power and purpose. These are the young women who will challenge their families and communities in order to make what is too often abstract Senegalese law a lived reality. Their force is still new, their futures unwritten and unknown—but imagining who these girls might become is thrilling.

Yet it is not the girls who most fascinate me during my time in Senegal. Time and again, as violence against African women is decried in these public forums, I find myself drawn to the faces of the older women in our midst. Some are local community leaders, seated, at the invitation of FAWE or World Vision, at the front of the classrooms. Others are anonymous faces in the crowds, their brows furrowing and their heads nodding as Adama speaks of the physical and psychological damage done to those who have lived through abuse. A handful of others came forward to share their own stories of living through violence, stories that are at once heartbreaking and hopeful because these women are still here, insisting on being seen and heard, so that what had been done to them will not be done to their daughters or granddaughters. In the faces of these older women, I discern something on which the hopes of the Senegalese girls can be built: the desire for vindication, which is perhaps its own form of hope.

For women in Senegal who've already suffered rape, incest, forced marriage, or cutting, it is far too late for a perfect justice. The violence visited on them, and the anguish that such violence most often leaves in its wake, informs their lives every day. Yet the world—their world, their own nation—is finally acknowledging what generations of West African women have known through their own painful, lived experience. The look I see on the faces of these older women listening to each antiviolence speaker during our tour tells a powerful story: their private burden had become a public mission. They are no longer alone.

One such person is an older woman I'll call Binata, a local leader who joins us at the Mandadouane school. During an informal and unguarded moment after a classroom presentation, Binata shares her story of surviving rape and female genital cutting with a small group of women from our delegation (thankfully, one of these women is an interpreter). Binata's reason for speaking is simple: "Now the children must hear." She seems to gain confidence as she speaks, and we in turn gain strength from listening to her. Soon her words usher in our own words, and a dialogue between four very different women, from three generations, begins. Despite our linguistic differences—or perhaps even because of them—the conversation flourishes. Our common ground, which is the fact that each of us has experienced violence or abuse in some form, transcends any differences. It is ground that women the world over have walked for centuries, often alone.

When we say our final good-byes that evening, Binata says to me in French, "*Ce fut une bonne journee*," which means, simply, "This was a good day." I nod and hug her, but in my sad, cynical heart, I am troubled by the inadequacy of it all: a single good day, or a thousand such days, could never make up for all she had endured. And yet she is right, it has been a good day. And a good day can sometimes be enough.

Our ability to be transformed by social change does not fade with time or age. If anything, our need for such transformation becomes more insistent as the accumulation of memory and grief presses upon us. "When I finally shared my truth, over thirty years after I was raped, I was in my fifties," says Janet Goldblatt Holmes, a dancer from Barrie, Ontario. "My decision to speak was prompted by seeing other women who had the courage to share, and it changed me completely. Today, when I hear younger women speaking out with a freedom I never felt I had at their age, what do I feel? Joy, and gratitude."

If it is true that it is never too late to be transformed by the power of a story, it is also true that there is no statute of limitations on our ability to become a transformer. In 1991, Florence Holway, a seventy-six-year-old painter living in Alton, New Hampshire, was raped in her home. When the twenty-five-year-old man who had attacked her was given a twelve-year sentence as part of a plea deal that Florence was never consulted on, her anger became a catalyst for her action.

"The terrible thing about this is not what happened to me, although that was bad enough," Florence told me when I met her in 2004. "It was that practically nothing was done to keep this from happening again. Well, this little old great-grandmother is going to change that." Today, thanks to a fight that Florence took all the way to her state legislature (and waged well into her eighties) sex offenders in New Hampshire are given longer mandatory sentences, and prosecutors cannot offer plea bargains without the victim's knowledge.

Janet Goldblatt Holmes

That's the thing about social change. It benefits the next generation, and the generation after that, until someday it is no longer recognized as change at all—it just *is*. We work to make the world better for our children, and to imagine the future as a kinder, more just place. Perhaps we invest so heavily in the next generation because real change, in real time, often seems to be an impossible dream. "The arc of the moral universe is long, but it bends toward justice," Dr. Martin Luther King Jr. famously said. His lovely words, though full of promise, have always seemed somehow sad to me—a reminder that those who most deserve to see justice in their own time too often know it only as a hope, rather than as a lived thing.

Sometimes, of course, it's both. A few years ago, I sat in a light-filled nursery and talked to Michelle de la Calle, a San Jose, California-based nurse. She had given birth to Julian, her infant son, over a month earlier. As she held him in her arms, we talked about her hopes for his future and for her own.

Michelle was raped when she was seventeen, and for the first year after the attack, she avoided talking about it because she worried that her story might make others uncomfortable. But the silence left her feeling isolated and unable to ask for the support she needed. So she began to speak—and quickly realized that refusing to remain silent made her feel stronger. She's continued to speak out over the last twenty years for a reason that is bigger than she is.

"I share my story to break the taboo around sexual violence," says Michelle. "And I share my story because I want other survivors to know that they can live on. Someday, my son will hear and understand my story. If that helps him grow up to be a man who respects women—that's a great reason to talk about rape, too."

Timeless: **Helen Finch**

Helen Finch is utterly composed. I am awkward and idiotic.

We are seated at a table at her favorite Santa Monica Mexican restaurant on a better-than-perfect—even for Southern California— spring day. She doesn't know it, but she is the first sexual violence survivor I am interviewing for *Lived Through This* (she is actually the first person I have ever interviewed, period, but why quibble about details). I come to our meeting believing I'm well prepared, and I'm quickly proven wrong. My Moleskine notebook has burrowed into the farthest reaches of my purse. I drop my pen on the floor. The table next to us, where an unidentifiable celebrity seems to be sitting, requests that I not use my tape recorder—a mild relief since the device feels at that moment utterly intimidating.

Helen watches me, smiles gently—pityingly?—and reassures me that "We have all the time in the world." And then she lifts her head ever so slightly, catches the waitress's eye, and says, "We'll need a pitcher of margaritas."

That gesture is pure Helen: easygoing and understanding, with plenty of joie de vivre mixed in. Over the next few hours, as we finish that pitcher of margaritas and more chips and guacamole than is ever advisable, I witness that joy at close range. Everything about Helen— the bell-ring of her laugh, her girlish habit of clasping her hands together when she is pleased, the way that she hugs me, hard, when we part—is infectious. An hour or so into that initial lunch, Helen smiles and says, "Young lady, I think I'd like to be in this book." It feels like a benediction (and she gets an extra nod for that "young lady").

Helen Lucile Finch was born in Los Angeles in 1913, and she's spent most of her life in California. She says that the weather, the openness, and the good fishing—a lifelong passion of Helen's—all suit her. Even from an early age, there was something fearless about her. Long before there was a Danica Patrick, Helen raced cars "right along with the boys." She tells me, with a certain pride, that she was sometimes mistaken for Amelia Earhart, who lived for a time in Helen's neighborhood (in photos the two women do bear a striking resemblance to one another). Helen is the kind of woman who never settles down, but instead settles in, comfortably, to each new stage of her life. She married her husband Mark, had a much-anticipated son, Dennis, and then lived decades of what she calls an "ordinary, mostly wonderful California life."

Helen was eighty-two years old when she was raped. She and Mark were in their car, not far from their Santa Monica home, when they were carjacked by an armed man. He forced Mark into the car's trunk, robbed the couple, and raped Helen repeatedly. Helen speaks about the violence she endured doing those hours with a candor I have rarely witnessed. She wants you to know that she was raped, but she also wants you to know what it feels like to be raped: the terror, the degradation, the physical discomfort, that horrible sense that it might never end, or that it might end fatally. For her, openness is a panacea and a mission. "If we can't talk about it, how will they know it is happening?" Helen asks. "How will it ever stop?"

Helen and Mark survived that night physically, reported the crime to the police, and "did what the experts told us you have to do when this happens," Helen says. "We just wanted them to catch him and make sure he didn't do it again. And we wanted to feel safe." That sense of safety proved elusive for Helen—and for Mark. "At first, I thought time would heal it, but feeling safe is one thing you don't get back," Helen says.

Helen turns serious—and speaks a bit more quietly—when she talks about the effect all of this had on her husband, who died of cancer two years after the attack. "I don't think Mark ever did get over my being raped," Helen says. "It ate him up inside.

"Mark is—he was—the kind of person who couldn't talk about that night, ever," Helen continues. "He died without ever really talking about what had happened to me, and to us. He was so private. He would say to me that I shouldn't tell people as much as I did, and still do, about being raped. But holding it in is a horrible thing."

It took four years for the police to find and arrest a suspect in Helen's case. When they finally did so, the accused was, not surprisingly, a repeat offender who would ultimately be sentenced to life in yet another rape case. At a preliminary hearing, Helen, who was called to testify, saw, for the first time, one of the other victims, a much younger woman, Julie,* who had been raped under circumstances much like Helen's. As Julie left the courtroom, she passed Helen, then eighty-six years old and on her way in to testify. Helen balled her hand into a fist and raised it in the air, signaling victory to Julie as they passed each other.

"There was something triumphant about Helen," Julie says. "There still is. To have gone through what she went through and to have that energy at her age; to be able to smile under these unbelievably difficult circumstances—that just amazed me." What Helen remembers about their first interaction is how natural smiling felt to her. "You go through this and then for years, nothing," Helen says. "You don't know if there will ever be justice. And then it happens, and they find someone, and it is wonderful."

It is a little-known fact that victims who have been raped by the same defendant cannot make contact until he has been sentenced or acquitted. So that encounter outside the courtroom remained, for some time, the extent of Julie and Helen's friendship. Neither of them positively identified their rapist at the hearing that day— "I didn't want to say it was him and have it turn out to be another fellow," explains Helen—but the district attorney, armed with additional evidence, moved forward with the prosecution.

A year later, Julie and Helen spoke for the first time in the district attorney's office. "There was such an amazing connection between us, a shared history that no one else could understand," says Julie. Helen remembers being struck by the range of women who had suffered at the hands of this rapist. "Women in their thirties, forties, all the way to me, in my eighties," says Helen. "We were all at risk."

*Not her real name.

At the trial of her assailant, the judge refused to utter the word *rape* at any point during the proceedings. "It was as if the word was too shameful to cross his lips," says Helen. "And I thought to myself, 'If I am almost ninety years old and can say the word *rape*, you have no excuse!'"

An additional piece of evidence emerged that still stuns Helen. Six years earlier—when Julie had first asked the police to let her look through hundreds of lineup photographs—she had correctly identified the man who went on to rape Helen. Despite Julie's identification, it took the police four years to question him and six years to gather enough evidence to bring the case to trial.

With the man who had raped them behind bars, Julie asked Helen if they could meet. They have been friends ever since. "We call each other 'mother and daughter by choice,'" Helen says. Their friendship may be grounded in past trauma, but today it is most characterized by long lunches, private-joke-sharing, and their shared love of fishing. They stay off the topic of politics. "She's a Democrat, and I'm a Republican," Helen says. "But we get on just fine."

Helen Finch understands what it means to grieve. She says that a trifecta of events have most profoundly shaped her life: the loss of her son Dennis, who died when he was just twenty-six, the rape she survived in 1995, and her husband's death from cancer two years later. During the time that I spend with Helen, she lives honestly and openly in her grief, talking about her past without losing sight of what she loves in her present. "If we don't go on living, they may as well have killed us," she tells me.

Helen's words—so simple, so true—have become a mantra for me. I have found myself saying them when, for whatever reason, the pain of my own past feels especially heavy. But it's not just her words I recall, it's Helen's essence. In my mind's eye, I can see her saying them to me—her hands clasped, her eyes open wide, her head nodding insistently. She is, each time I see her, vividly alive.

One of Helen's secrets, I conclude, is her compassion. When I tell her how sorry I am that she was raped at such a vulnerable life stage, she tells me that she is sorry that I was raped when I was so very young. "Anne, I had over eighty years before I was raped," Helen says. "I am just so sorry that you will have to live with these memories for so long. It's not right." That, in some basic sense is Helen: leaping out of her own pain and into someone else's, recognizing that even in her grief, she is not alone.

A year after I first meet her, I am invited to Helen's ninetieth birthday party at Yamashiro, a Japanese restaurant high in the Hollywood Hills (the photo at the start of this chapter was taken at the celebration). It's a clear, cool, early June evening, and as the sun sets on the party, Helen is in fine form. There is cake, there is champagne, and there are gifts, including a proclamation in Helen's honor signed by the mayor of Santa Monica. "I don't think much of him," Helen says with a laugh. "But it's a nice enough gesture."

Author's note: Helen Finch passed away on February 17, 2008. She is missed.

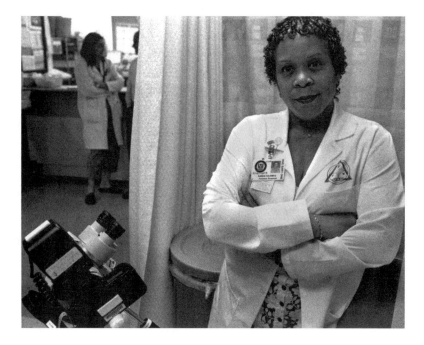

The Safe Zone: **Karen Carroll**

Karen Carroll was stunned.

Stunned when her husband of four years threatened her with a knife ("I knew he had anger issues, but I never thought he was capable of that"). Stunned when, having secured an order of protection against him, she woke on a Saturday morning and saw his outline in the door of her bedroom, faint at first, and then terrifyingly familiar. And stunned, in the worst way possible, when he gagged, beat, and raped her, a series of messages masquerading as violent acts: *You do not matter. You do not belong to yourself. You won't live if you speak up again.*

All of this shocked and devastated Karen. And then, after her estranged husband had fled, the police had been called, and Karen was taken to the emergency department of a Yonkers, New York, hospital, she was stunned again.

Karen's superficial bruises and cuts had been treated, and she was waiting, alone, for the doctor who was to perform her sexual assault examination. Karen remembers her feeling of vulnerability as she waited for that doctor. "I felt so alone in there," Karen says. "It was a room that I would have described as 'ordinary' before the rape—but it just seemed sterile and cold to me as I sat there looking at everything."

A male doctor walked into the examining room and shut the door. He did not greet Karen. He did not even look at her. Instead, he turned to the counter, picked up the rape kit—a box containing everything needed to gather and preserve the physical evidence left on the victim—and began to read the instructions. He seemed annoyed. He seemed—though Karen is not sure about this—disgusted. He was clearly unfamiliar with the rape exam process.

"I went from humiliated to hurt to 'Oh my God, what if he screws this up and my husband goes free,' in about ninety seconds," Karen says with a tiny laugh that becomes, very quickly, a sigh. "And I convinced him to let me help him."

As coincidence—or "providence," the word Karen prefers—would have it, at the time she was raped, Karen was the head emergency room nurse at Yonkers General Hospital, a few miles away. Karen was not well-versed in rape evidence collection, but she was fairly confident that she would do a better job than the confused and oddly indifferent doctor in that examining room.

"The funny thing is that when the police first came to my home, I had asked them not to take me to Yonkers General because I wanted to be professional, to have boundaries," Karen says. "I didn't want one of my colleagues to have to treat me. And yet there I was, treating myself."

Karen is careful not to downplay the trauma of being raped and beaten by her husband. But for her, the memory of that emergency room experience has been almost as painful (and absolutely as lasting).

"Violence is horrible and confusing," Karen says. "You expect violence to be horrible and confusing. But the hospital? That's supposed to be the place where it starts to get better, where things feel under control, and that was not what happened to me."

During the first year after she was raped, Karen was living what she calls a "pretend life"—acting as if everything was fine, while knowing that it was anything but. It took six weeks for Karen's estranged husband to be caught and arrested (he ultimately served seven years for the crimes he committed that night). During those first weeks, she saw his face in every car that drove past her, and felt panic each time she heard footsteps behind her on the street. "I had had an order of protection," Karen says, "and look what he had done with that."

Karen rarely slept—and when she did, it was only with the lights and the TV on. Nights were the worst, and days were only made possible because her nursing job kept her so busy that she "couldn't think, thank God."

Karen had always loved her work—she prided herself on her professionalism—but doing her job really well was difficult. "You think you'll be able to do it," Karen says. "And then you're in the middle of a medical crisis, and a millions things are coming at you, and you realize, 'OK, that's why they invented a good night's sleep.'"

Karen shared the fact that she had been raped with her coworkers and family—"I had to, because they needed to know that if my ex-husband showed up, he was a danger"—but she didn't want to talk about the experience in any detail. One reason for this was her desire to protect her two adolescent sons (their father was her first husband and not the man who had raped her). "I had been working so hard to raise them to be good men, to expose them to strong male role models," says Karen. "I needed to protect them from this."

Somehow, sharing the details of her story with strangers was easier. "After they caught my husband, I had to talk about the rape with the assistant district attorney, the police, lots of people I did not know," says Karen. "But I almost never talked about it to the people I was close to. I was not there yet."

Karen believes that her initial discomfort with sharing her story was shaped by her family history. Her mother had been a domestic violence victim, and watching her being abused was one of the most difficult aspects of Karen's own childhood. Karen remembers feeling "all of the love and sympathy in the world for my mother," coupled with a strong belief that this would never, ever happen to her.

"When you have that pride that you'd never let any man do that to you, and then you're raped by your own husband, you feel so much," Karen says. "Shame. Shock. Having to face that you are not so different after all."

"It took me a long time to realize that it wasn't about me, or my mother, or any other woman. It was about the men who did this to us."

Karen is a woman who believes that everything happens for a reason—someone who takes comfort in her sense that we are part of a grand plan. After she was raped, she was vexed by a simple, impossible question: "Why me?"

"There is no reason. I know that," Karen says. "But I needed to find a purpose. Then I realized that this didn't happen to me because of something I had done. It happened to me because of what I was *going to do*."

What Karen most wanted to do was combine her love of nursing—"even during that first bad year, I never lost that love for taking care of people"—and her painfully earned knowledge about what too often happens to rape victims in emergency rooms.

After she was raped, Karen had begun to hear from other survivors who had had difficult experiences at the hands of EMTs, nurses, doctors, and other first responders. She is careful to point out that most emergency room doctors and nurses are "amazing, dedicated, good people." But she knows that without training and experience, it can be very easy for things to go wrong.

"Not every bad experience is like mine," Karen says. "There are nurses who are excellent at evidence collection but don't know how to talk to victims. There are nurses who are great with victims but have not had training in evidence collection. I wanted to do both."

So Karen went back to school at Columbia University and trained to become a sexual assault nurse examiner (SANE). She has been working as a SANE ever since. She says that her experience was an advantage for her during her schooling. "I was no longer the woman I had been before I was raped," Karen says, "which was a good thing. I had a knowledge and compassion that they could not teach me."

Karen believes that most people—even many in law enforcement—don't always understand that the stakes are as high in the medical exam rooms as they are for the police officers who gather evidence at the scene of the crime.

"So many of these cases are lost on evidence collection," Karen says. "If a SANE screws up during the sexual assault exam and doesn't collect that DNA, some rapist goes free. It's that simple." But for Karen, the job is about compassion as much as competence. She understands that a victim's body is a crime scene. But as a nurse, she never loses sight of the fact that that body belongs to a human being.

"When I see a victim at what is probably the worst moment in her life, she is going to hear this from me: 'I believe you, and I'm sorry,'" Karen says. "That's not what I do before I start my job doing the examination. That's *part* of the job."

Karen believes that one of America's biggest public safety challenges is the national backlog of untested rape kits—over four hundred thousand of them currently languish in evidence collection facilities across the country. Each kit includes the DNA evidence that nurses like Karen collect during the sexual assault examination—evidence that can point the police in the direction of an assailant, be used to successfully prosecute a rapist at trial, or crack open a cold case.

Karen first spoke out about the rape kit backlog in 2002 when she joined New York congresswoman Carolyn Maloney at a press conference calling for national funding for forensic nurse programs and DNA testing for backlogged rape kits. She's been active on the issue ever since. In 2013, as part of the re-authorization of the Violence Against Women Act, President Obama signed the Sexual Assault Forensic Evidence Registry (SAFER) Act into law, putting the power of funding behind the government's pledge to eliminate the backlog.

It's what Karen, and thousands of others in the criminal justice and public health fields, have been calling for for more than a decade. "When a survivor takes that courageous step to come forward, and a SANE does her job and collects that DNA, our government owes it to them both to do something with it," Karen says.

Today, Karen is the associate director of the Bronx Sexual Assault Response Team (SART), where she creates collaborations between police, EMTs, SANEs, and prosecutors. Whenever she shares her expertise as a nurse, she also shares her personal story. "I left the shame behind years ago," Karen says. "But I leave it behind all over again every time I say, 'Yes, this happened to me.'"

Paying It Forward: **Katie Feifer**

The first thing you notice about Katie Feifer is her abundant, reddish-brown, never-been-straightened shock of curls. "Tell Katie to send me one-eighth of her beautiful hair," laughed a mutual friend recently. "She'll never miss it, and it will do me a world of good!"

She was raised in Oak Park, a suburb outside of Chicago, an only child born when her mom was in her forties. She describes her home as "absolutely loving—my parents, and especially my dad, spoiled me rotten. He made me feel that the sun rose and set on me. And I bought into the belief that I could do no wrong." If there is a case to be made for the notion that behind every strong and smart woman is a doting father, Katie Feifer might be "Exhibit A."

After attending a small, private liberal arts college, she landed her first job, in the research department at one of the world's largest advertising agencies. Katie remembers her mother, a proud feminist, warning her not to let on that she could type because the company would have Katie doing the work of a secretary. She didn't do much typing. Eight short years and six promotions later, she became the youngest vice president in the company's history. "In research, I had a career that used all my skills: part sociology, part psychology, part diplomacy, part sales," says Katie.

When Katie was thirty-one, author Lisa Birnbach profiled her in *Going to Work*, a best-selling book about interesting companies and the equally interesting people who work in them. "I was embarrassed about it at the time, but I kind of liked it," laughs Katie now. "I was a middle-class suburban kid, born to a Socialist mom and a liberal Democrat dad who didn't trust the system, and somehow I landed this great corporate job. I felt completely unflappable, totally accomplished. I loved my work. I loved my friends. With the money I was making, I bought a house in Oak Park, a suburb just outside of Chicago. OK, so my love life sucked—it was a big mess that could be a book in itself. But overall, I had a really good life."

That good life changed on the evening of September 15, 1988, when a member of a work crew painting Katie's home rang her doorbell and told her he had left a sweater inside her home earlier in the day. He was all of seventeen, "a skinny white kid, if I had to describe him," notes Katie, "but look, I was a woman living alone, so it never occurred to me to even consider letting him in. So I told him no and that I was going to have to call his boss to confirm his story. I shut the door, which I remember gave me some feeling of relief, but when I went to phone his boss, he broke into the house, and this time he had a knife. It was weird because the whole thing had shifted. He was the one telling me what to do, and believe me, when there is a knife involved, you are going to do what you are told to do. After he raped me, he left me tied and gagged in the basement. I felt so much panic when he did that; I am a very verbal person and losing my voice was horrible. And that was it. I felt like I had died—but I lived. My whole life just changed."

Katie managed to free herself and call 911. A male detective and a female beat officer arrived and called an ambulance before taking down some basic information about the attack. Later that night, after being released from the hospital, Katie returned to the police station to give a more detailed statement to the same male detective who had been there. He had been made the lead officer on the case. When asked about her experience with the police, Katie says, "Every contact I had with that lead officer was positive. Every one. He was great, supportive, my knight in shining armor. He made me feel safe immediately after the attack, and he made me feel safe later. I remember that a day after the rape, I received a flower delivery that freaked me out—any sort of delivery person, anyone ringing my doorbell, was terrifying after the rape—and he came back to my house to reassure me that everything was OK.

"He acted like it was the most normal thing in the world for a woman to be hysterical because someone was trying to send her flowers," Katie says. "Here's the thing. He never doubted me, never made me think it was my fault. He just seemed to get it, to know what I was going through emotionally. To me, this one man was the police, and he was perfect."

That these are words rarely spoken by other rape survivors is not lost on Katie. She knows that in this aspect, her story is all too rare. She also knows that this single moment—that first time that she voiced the words "I was raped" to the officers who met her at the scene of the crime—was in fact a defining moment, one that set in motion an openness that she believes was at the core of whatever healing she has experienced in the years since. "I had a horrible thing happen, but the thing about it was people believed me. And that was everything to me. I did not have to live with the horror of being doubted, and that started with the very first officers on the scene, who left me with no doubt that they knew that every word I was saying was true. Something about my upbringing, maybe my mom's feminism, gave me an immediate sense that I should not be ashamed. The responses of the police reinforced that openness. I think that if I had not been believed the very first time I told the officers what had happened to me, I might not have been able to be open again."

Thanks in large part to the description Katie gave, the police were able to catch her rapist within hours of her assault. She identified him in a lineup that very same night. He confessed, was arrested, and was put in jail before Katie went home. Ultimately, in a plea negotiation, he was sentenced to fifteen years for the rape.

He served only six. "You have to understand: he was seventeen, he looked nothing like a criminal, it was 1988, and they thought this was the best they could do," Katie says now. Since even today, the average sentence served by convicted rapists in this country is still less than five and a half years, there is a regrettable logic to the decision.

When asked about her experience with the criminal justice system, Katie says that it was largely positive. "The state's attorney who prosecuted my rape was wonderful, kind, nice to me. My phone calls were returned. My questions were answered. I was consulted about accepting that plea negotiation instead of taking the case to trial, and I agreed to it before they did anything. I was treated with dignity."

I ask Katie about her life in the weeks and months after the assault, and her story—despite the validations of a system that more often than not seems to invalidate rape victims—converges with those of many women. "I kept my job, but I wasn't very functional at work," notes Katie. "I took time off, left early, and sometimes just sat in my office not working. I couldn't sleep. I was going to stay in my home. I had just bought that house. But nights were so difficult. So my next-door neighbors would let me come over to their home every night, at ten or eleven, and I'd sleep there. The next morning, after having coffee with them, I'd head home and get ready for work. Looking back, it was an amazing thing that they did. They were so good to me.

"For a while, I thought I would have to quit my job. I had been this huge achiever, and it wasn't happening anymore. The therapist I was seeing helped me understand that I was used to being competent and powerful on the job, but I had felt so powerless in being raped that I was trying desperately to resolve that dissonance by proving that I also wasn't powerful at work. Believe me, I wasn't, but I kept telling myself that I had to accept that everything I was feeling was a normal reaction to a totally abnormal trauma, and that it was OK. That did help, because I did not feel 'normal.' I went through a stage of being obsessed with true crime books, reading them until three or four in the morning. I had never been that interested in these books before, but I felt a total identification with other crime victims. I was terrified when I saw young white guys, alone or in groups. It made going to the mall, walking down certain streets, so scary for me. I had a bizarre fear when I was stopped in rush-hour traffic that a person in the car next to me was going to shoot me—that I was going to die in the next minute. So my morning commute was a nightmare of tension for me."

"I cried all the time, privately and publicly, and you have to understand, I was the kind of woman people thought was strong. I did think briefly of suicide—it was incredibly difficult to keep going with so much anxiety—but my therapist helped me through it. Her office and our sessions were an oasis for me, I needed that place to go every week to talk. I broke up with my boyfriend of twelve years.

It was a relationship that probably should have ended eleven years before, and the rape brought it to a head. I think that rape does that. Whatever is not working in your life really doesn't work after you've been attacked. What else? Well, I ate a lot of chocolate!" Katie says with a laugh.

Katie remembers, vividly, the day a coworker told her that she, too, had been raped. "She didn't say much, but somehow just knowing that she had gone through this made talking to her natural and easy, and she became someone I could go to. Even early on, there was so much power in sharing, especially with other women who had been raped. I remember when one day I went sobbing into her cubicle because I couldn't work, she just said, 'Katie, go home. Lie on your couch with a blanket over you and come back when you can. It's okay to do that. Don't try to tough it out.' Just having permission to bail on that one shitty day gave me what I needed."

It's those acts of kindness that had the biggest effect on Katie, and her clear memories of the smallest gestures underscore their transformative power. She remembers the CEO of her company, who gave her a key to the corporate garage and her own parking space, a privilege usually reserved for top executives; the boss who offered to bus in enough people to fill the courtroom to support Katie on the day that her rapist was sentenced; her friend Ray, who offered to come over to wash the windows because Katie was afraid to allow anyone she didn't know to work at her home.

And she remembers the girlfriend who responded immediately when Katie called her, crying, from the gym because she was certain that a young, skinny white kid was following her. "She didn't ask a single question when I called," Katie says. She just drove to the gym, calmed me down in the locker room, and walked me to my own car. So many people, so many supportive actions. A lot of them were little things. Acceptance, compassion, kindness, and thoughtfulness. That was all. And it was everything."

It was certainly enough to cement a powerful belief in the generosity of the world around her, a belief that was invaluable fifteen years after her rape, when Katie received a surprising call from the deputy district attorney in Las Vegas. What the DDA told Katie that day still stuns and wounds her, for she heard for the first time about the life her rapist had lived since leaving prison in 1995. Older and hardened even further, he had committed a string of crimes in the Midwest, before heading across the country to Las Vegas, where he murdered the father of a fifteen-year-old girl.

Convinced that Katie's testimony about her rape years earlier was key to the sentencing phase of the trial, the DDA appealed to her to testify. Frightened, but absolutely convinced that it was the thing she had to do, Katie flew to Las Vegas to again face her attacker. "I only looked at him once—when I was asked to face him and tell the court that yes, he was the man who had raped me all those years ago. I almost literally couldn't stomach it. Not because his face reminded me of the attack. I knew it was him, but he looked different to me. The suit he was wearing, the aging—he was in his thirties—the hardness of the eyes, a grimness that wasn't there in quite the same way when he was seventeen.

"I had had fantasies about confronting him, but when I had the chance, I did not want to look at him," says Katie, "and that made me think about what it must be like for women who are raped by men they know, what it must be like to have to live with their rapists, to work with them, to go to school with them." It is one of Katie's many moments of identification with other survivors, an identification that takes in the essential inhumanity of sexual violence in all its forms—on dates and in dorm rooms, at the hands of strangers, and even those we love—and seems to expand, rather than contract, Katie's world.

In recalling the feeling of facing her attacker after so many years, Katie says, "I was shocked at how visceral my reactions were. When I spoke of how he made me feel dead, I clutched my heart and my stomach. When I talked about being gagged, my fingers kept touching and covering my lips."

It is painful to think of Katie this way—covering her own mouth—cast back, if only for that moment, into the lonely world that is silence. But Katie, who is as free of that world as any survivor I have known, did not remain silent. She testified at length that day, and in the wake of her words—clear, unflinching, speaking truth to both power and perpetrator—her rapist, already convicted of murder, was sentenced to death. Then and now, the prosecutor on the case is certain that Katie's testimony was what swayed the jury, convincing them that this murder was not an isolated evil, but the most recent event in a long history of brutality. "Without question, Katie's testimony was the most powerful piece of evidence," he now says.

Katie acknowledges her complex, though not conflicted, beliefs about the death sentence he received for committing murder. "I struggled with my feelings about the death penalty before I testified. It affected me very strongly, that feeling that I would be playing a role in having someone sentenced to die. I don't want the state to kill its citizens, and I value life above all. It is sacred, and miraculous—every life is a gift, and I am appalled by how disproportionately the death penalty is applied to those who are poor or black. But for me, the paramount consideration is the safety of society. There is no doubt about my rapist's guilt in that murder, and no doubt about his inability to live in society without seriously harming people. So, as abhorrent as the death penalty is, it is better than having this man or others like him, harm anyone else."

When asked if her experience after her own rape—when the system and so many of her friends, family, and colleagues had responded to her needs—had made it easier for her to answer the call to testify, Katie answers emphatically. "Yes, yes, yes, yes, yes!! I felt that I would do anything to help the DA because of how many people helped me. I do think it's that simple. I wanted to pay back. I wanted to pay forward. I really believed in that."

It has been said that "there are no small acts of kindness," but this phrase has always seemed inadequate somehow: an attempt to infuse the personal with qualities of the political, the way we convince ourselves that small actions, as opposed to larger activism, can change the world. And yet, in those moments and months after Katie Feifer was raped, a series of often small gestures (undoubtedly the result of education, training, and that most elusive of qualities, genuine compassion) came together to not only sustain Katie, but to move her forward.

Years later, Katie was able to turn back, in search of a justice that would last longer than six years, in hopes of stopping a violent man from doing again what he had done to her. Today someone, somewhere, is safe and well, doing the most ordinary of things—taking out the trash, complaining to a coworker, dressing the kids for school—because Katie Feifer was willing to do the extraordinary.

And where is Katie now? She is the owner of her own research firm, happily married to her partner, Ric, and the proud mother of Shira, a twenty-year-old college student. Katie also volunteers as a SART member and is a founding member of CounterQuo, a national initiative that challenges legal and media response to rape. In the hours and days I've spent with her, in long chats about her rape and so much more, Katie is open about the trauma and grief of her experience, yet utterly in possession of the event. I never see her cry.

Then one day, as Katie and I share the sort of intimate conversation that emerges when two rape survivors come together in that space where real understanding flourishes, I ask her what she thinks it would have been like for her if she hadn't been heard and believed and supported so many times, by so many people. She looks down, as her hand moves near her mouth, and she is silent for a long moment. I do not remember her, before or since, ever being so silent, and when she finally looks up at me, the tears have moved past her eyes and onto her face. She is not crying, but weeping. "I don't know," Katie says slowly. "I honestly do not know what would have happened to me."

Front row: Colleen MacQuarrie
Middle (left to right): Melissa Good, Annie Nielson, Judy Donovan Whitty
Back (left to right): Katie Whalen, Pat Sobey, Gladys Kenny

That Sense of Place:
The Survivors of
Prince Edward Island

In travel, as in much of life, reality rarely lives up to the ideal. We fall in love with a place in outline: its look, its location, the promise that it will be something different (and that we will be different once we're there). Then we arrive at our destination and fill in that outline with details—the intricacies and intimacies of a region, the things that bring us closer to its truth.

I first visited Prince Edward Island, a Canadian maritime province, when I was eleven years old. That trip was part family vacation, part young girl's pilgrimage to a literary Lourdes. The island was made famous by *Anne of Green Gables*, Lucy Maude Montgomery's classic 1908 children's story about a red-haired, eleven-year-old, orphan girl who comes to live on a farm there during the Victorian era. *Anne of Green Gables* is a classic (it has sold over fifty million copies worldwide) and a clarion call. I defy you to read the book without wanting to visit the island where the story is set.

The Anne in *Anne of Green Gables* is the original young-adult heroine, Prince Edward Island's very own "new girl." She is smart, she is charming, but most of all she is *unusual*. She precociously pushes the limits of language. She is uninterested in the resident cute boy. She is tempted, at book's end, to leave home, but remains dutifully and happily on the island instead.

Lucy Maude Montgomery—the book's author, who was Prince Edward Island-born and raised—has rendered this place so vividly that it becomes her book's secondary character. It's pastoral and pristine, with white sand beaches, winding red dirt roads, and a community of small-town characters who are charming, sometimes quirky, but invariably *good*. The novel is a love letter to rural small-town values, an argument, in child-friendly prose, that there are places that are too good to ever leave.

In my Chicago suburban adolescent eyes, and in my parents' opinion, Prince Edward Island, circa the late nineteen seventies, lived up to its literary hype. It was one of our favorite family vacation destinations, a place with people who were so friendly that you never went anywhere without being greeted, and so easygoing that they seemed to be saying, collectively, *just breathe*. And my Dad could fish there.

Decades later, I visit Prince Edward Island again, this time on a very different sort of pilgrimage. The Voices and Faces Project was expanding its efforts into Canada, and we were invited to come to the island to share a series of sexual violence survivor stories from our documentary initiative. "We want you to talk about rape and abuse to help us raise public awareness," Sigrid Rolfe, the organizational coordinator at the Prince Edward Island Sexual Assault Centre, said. "But if you can stay and listen, that might make an even bigger difference."

In many ways, the Prince Edward Island I return to feels unchanged. It is still gorgeous, still friendly, still smells of the Atlantic, and is now—cottage industries being what they are—an even more impressive mecca for *Anne of Green Gables* lovers. But during this trip, I am introduced to a different side of the island.

At the Prince Edward Island Sexual Assault Centre, I spend an afternoon with seven members of an island antiviolence collective called SAGE. These women clearly know one another well—when I first walk into the center's cozy meeting room, I interrupt a group conversation about grandchildren, while Melissa Good and Katie Whalen, two of the younger SAGE members, stand to the side discussing the statement-making power of getting a tattoo.

The SAGE women are different ages and at different life stages. Their point of connection is that they are each survivors of childhood sexual abuse who are using their stories to challenge the island community they clearly love. Every one of them was raped or sexually assaulted by someone she knows.

"We live in one of the most beautiful places on earth," says Pat Sobey, a founding member of SAGE. "But bad things happen to good people, even in places like this."

Over the course of the next three hours, the truths these seven women tell are uneasy ones. They share stories of being sexually abused by a trusted neighbor, a foster brother, an uncle, an adored father. They talk about years spent believing that they were alone, and what it feels like to realize, at last, that they are not: *I used to look at other girls at church and wonder, you too? Now I look at the women in this room and know: You, too.*

They believe that childhood sexual abuse is a sort of plague that too often runs through families and generations on Prince Edward Island, leaving devastation—in the form of depression, substance abuse, apathy, or more violence—in its wake.

Pat Sobey was five years old when her foster brother sexually assaulted her. She says that it took her years to understand what had happened to her, to be able to match her pain to the word "abuse." "I saw my foster brother not long ago," Pat says. "And he said, 'We had so much fun back then.'"

"It had taken years for me to be able to say to him, 'You were fifteen. I was five. That was not fun, that was abuse,'" Pat says. She expected, or hoped, that "speaking truth" to her foster brother might provide some form of resolution for her. Instead, it brought her closer to what the SAGE women believe is a familiar cycle of violence. "He looked shocked when I called what he had done child abuse," Pat recalls. "And then he told me that he had been sexually abused growing up, too."

Pat's foster brother's response left her conflicted. "Most people who have been abused do not abuse someone else," she says firmly, "but it does show how childhood sexual abuse can start in one generation or person, get treated as ordinary, and then happen again if we don't break the cycle."

Judy Donovan Whitty, a mother of five and a grandmother of six—"please print that!"—says she is also sharing her story to raise awareness of generational cycles.

When she was growing up on Prince Edward Island in the nineteen fifties, her parents were local leaders who were beloved in her community. "If we had a mayor in our village, my father would have been it," Judy says quietly. "He was our choir director. He owned the local general store and provided credit for the poor. He helped the disabled.

All of those good qualities were real, but my father also began sexually abusing me at a very young age."

Judy still remembers the "intense shame" she felt when she told her parish priest, at the age of seven, what was happening in her home. The priest's response was devastating. "He told me that my father was a good man who would never have meant to hurt me," Judy says, "and he told me that I had sinned. 'Judy, that was your very own father! You must not let that happen again.'"

Judy says that she is past wondering what might have been different for her if that priest had responded with compassion, or taken action on her behalf. Instead, her father continued to abuse Judy until she was an adolescent, and Judy continued to blame herself for the abuse. In the nineteen nineties—Judy was then in her forties—an unrelated family crisis prompted her to finally come to terms with, and begin to share, the fact that she had been abused by her father. Counseling, and her husband's support, were both critical for Judy at that time. "Just having my husband say, 'I have faith in you, I believe you' helped me so much," Judy says. "Speaking out was the beginning of me healing the splinter in my heart."

With her husband's encouragement, Judy finally confronted her by-then elderly father. Somewhat to her surprise, Judy's father acknowledged that he had abused her, apologized for it, and asked for her forgiveness. He then told her that an uncle had sexually abused him when he was a young boy.

"That is not an excuse for what he did, and I don't think he thought it was, not at all," Judy says. "But it sure did help me understand a bit."

For Judy and for Pat, sharing their stories began as a way to come to terms with their personal histories. But as they became more open about having lived through childhood sexual abuse, they began, inevitably, to meet other survivors. Sometimes that happened informally over coffee with a neighbor who had her own story to tell. Other times, survivor paths crossed through the Prince Edward Island Sexual Assault Centre or other local service providers.

A new community of childhood sexual violence survivors was beginning to emerge on the island—a group of women who believed that their stories had personal, as well as political, power. In 2006, the SAGE collective—a group of island women with a mandate to educate the community on preventing and responding to childhood sexual abuse—was born (seven SAGE members were photographed for this book; there are more than a dozen other members on the island).

"We had always been there, with our silent stories," says Gladys Kenny, who has been involved with SAGE since its earliest days. "So many women on the island have. But coming out together as a group was safer, more powerful. If someone told me when I was eighteen that one day I would have the courage to speak out about being abused, I would never have believed it."

"Avoidance" is a word that comes up repeatedly during the time I spend with the SAGE women. What do people know? What should people know? Why do adults choose not to see things? What happens when adults do see, and still do nothing? These women are speaking out because they believe that to prevent child sexual abuse on Prince Edward Island, avoidance has to be replaced with accountability.

"If only I knew, I would have done something," is a phrase used often when adults learn of a case of childhood sexual violence. But the experiences of SAGE women I speak with seem to challenge that idea. To a woman they say that they tried, as children, to share their stories with someone—often with an adult family member or a figure of authority.

Some of them did so awkwardly, or in code—by insisting to their parents that they did not want to be around an adult family "friend," or by telling someone what "Daddy did" (and being told that it "must have been a dream"). Many of the SAGE women say that they changed so completely after living through violence—turning to drugs or alcohol or self-harm—that those changes should have served as red flags to any knowledgeable, or even just caring, adult around them.

"What I want is for adults to have an awareness," Melissa Good, a mother of three, says firmly. "Look a little deeper. Ask questions. Because our kids find a way to tell us their truths if we are paying attention."

Holding a child rapist accountable is rarely a single, simple act. It means exposing not only the individual who is abusing but also the system of thought that has allowed him or her to do so with impunity. And it means facing one of the most uncomfortable truths of all: the number of adults who might have done something, but didn't, the number of should-be protectors who managed to look away.

The SAGE women are painfully aware of this. "I was failed first by my abuser," Colleen MacQuarrie, another founding SAGE member, says, "and I was failed again by the adults who should have stopped it. And I won't let that happen to any child on my watch, not ever."

In *Unspoken Crimes: Sexual Assault in Rural America*, a 2003 study undertaken by the Centers for Disease Control and Prevention (CDC), researchers found that victims of rape or sexual abuse in rural or isolated areas often have greater difficulty disclosing than those in urban areas, especially in cases where the victim knows the perpetrator. They point to a series of "informal social codes" that encourage those who have been abused to remain silent in order to protect their family or trusted members of the community. And they look at how population density and high levels of familiarity can make it difficult for victims to come forward with any degree of anonymity.

Put another way, a rural community's virtues—*everyone knows your name, there are no strangers here, we know whom we can trust*—can turn on victims in the most painful ways. "Who do you go to for help when everyone who might help you knows your father?" Judy asks simply. "Where do you go if you don't want the whole town to know that you were raped? That's a very lonely feeling."

On my last day on Prince Edward Island, I spend an afternoon at the charmingly ramshackle Charlottetown farm where Mike Avery lives with his wife—his two sons are grown—and a menagerie of farm animals. Mike's three-legged mutt, Molson, rubs against my legs when I get out of the car. "He's broken, but we love him," Mike laughs as I extend my hand, and I like them both—Mike and his dog—immediately. Nirvana's "Nevermind" floats in from another room as we enter Mike's back door. He makes a pot of tea, then pushes aside a pile of mail, and we sit down at his laminated kitchen table to talk.

When he was eleven years old, Mike was raped by a neighbor, the son-in-law of a "good, kind farm couple" who lived nearby. "I was at their place, baling hay to earn some extra money," Mike says, "and he

Mike Avery

found me alone." Mike pauses, and then looks at his hands. "It's hard
to explain how something that's over in three minutes can change a
boy's whole life—but my God, it does."

It took Mike twenty-three years to talk about being raped. He
says that he had no idea where or how he might have found help
earlier. He finally shared his story when his substance abuse issues
became so serious that he felt that he needed to explain himself to
his wife and family. "I came from good parents, I had created a good
family of my own, and I did not want to lose that," Mike says. "I was
in this sea of insanity with a broken compass, and I had to tell my
wife, my parents, my kids: 'this is what broke my compass.'"

For Mike, speaking out led to seeking help. He says that counseling has been critical for him, and his willingness to be open about

his story encouraged other men on the island to speak. "I now know of three other victims who were raped by this person," Mike says. "There were probably many more. You feel bad about that. You don't want to be alone in this, but at the same time, you don't want it to have happened to anyone else."

Has speaking publicly been therapeutic for Mike? "It's pretty hard at times," Mike says. "Once you talk about it . . . This is a small town; everyone is going to know. But my family stands behind me. They know that I need to do this, because I want a different future for us, and every adult on this island has an obligation to try to stop child abuse in any way they can."

As he walks me to the car—Mike's horse, doing its best interpretation of a dog, trots behind us at close range—I ask Mike if he's ever wanted to leave Prince Edward Island or his farm. He looks surprised and turns to face me. "This is my home, Anne," he says, that lovely Canadian accent making his statement sound almost, but not quite, like a question. "These are my roots here. We're not going anywhere."

ACKNOWLEDGMENTS

Belief is at the heart of this book: the belief that Patricia Evans and I had in the power of the stories of survivors of sexual violence to create change, and the belief that so many people had in the two of us as we embarked on the journey that became *Lived Through This*. At the heart of this journey are the women and men who have shared their stories with us over the course of the last decade—not only those featured on these pages, but hundreds of others whose testimonies have informed our work. Thank you for your courage, your openness, and your trust.

This book was born of a simple idea and, as is often the case, a fierce group of women. The "Wednesday Team" at the Voices and Faces Project has been the driving force behind this project since we first came together in 2004. To Aimee Bravo-Noffsinger, Courtney Comer, Christa Desir, Katie Feifer, Xiomy Rodriguez-Fahs, Victoria Sherden, and Tracey Stevens: Know that for more reasons than I can ever list, this book would not exist without your amazing selves.

George Greenfield, my agent, has been similarly engaged in this project since its early days. His energy, his idealism, and his willingness to endure an endless string of calls that begin with "I have an idea" are just a few of the reasons he has so thoroughly endeared himself to me. The team at Beacon Press—led by my ever-patient editor, Amy Caldwell—has inspired me with their desire to make *Lived Through This* a book that encourages people to think, feel, and act. Early on, Matt McGowan, Ellen Geiger, Frances Goldin, and Priscilla Gilman also provided vital editorial suggestions; I am grateful for their contributions. The enthusiasm that Scott Berkowitz and Debbie Andrews had for *Lived Through This* during its earliest and most vulnerable stages was critical, and the belief of the entire team at RAINN has been a constant source of inspiration. And to Mary Hutchings Reed, Catherine Joyce, and the dedicated team at Winston & Strawn: your legal assistance, married to your passion for the creative arts, has been invaluable.

"When in doubt, listen to women," I have been told. Three extraordinary women have been my most trusted mentors over the course of this project: Bette Cerf Hill, who shows me, each time I am in her company, that curiosity is our greatest gift; Sunny Fischer, who lives her belief that ideas are only transformative when they are backed by hard work; and Vera Klement, whose art and life compel me in more ways than she perhaps knows.

A group of fellow warriors in the fight for human and women's rights especially informed my thinking as I wrote this book and became treasured friends along the way: Houston Baker, Kemery Bloom, Jimmie Briggs, April Donnellan, Rachel Durchslag, Barbara Engel, Maya Friedler, Donna Jenson, Stephanie Hanson, Lynne Johnson, Jamie Kalven, Laurel Lipkin, Brenda Myers-Powell, Georgia Murray, Jody Raphael, Jessie Mindlin, Stacey Malone, Marina Nemat, Charlotte Pierce-Baker, Randy Rosenberg, Leslie Thomas, Nancy Venable-Raine, and Susan Vickers.

I am indebted to Robin Smith, who gently reminded me—at a moment when I most needed reminding—that having my own story to share could be my greatest gift as a writer; to Jennifer Severns, Tracie Wagman, and Alisa Roadcup, for the hours of conversation that inspired "New Rules for Radicals"; to Kathe Telingator, a dear friend and astute reader rolled into one; to Leah Missbach Day and Julie Fedeli, who engaged an entire community of "goddesses" in *Lived Through This*; to Mónica Ramirez for her ever-present belief, love, and wisdom; and to Hannah Rosenthal and Isabel Stewart of the

Chicago Foundation for Women, Elizabeth Driehaus at the Richard H. Driehaus Foundation, Debra Crown Harriman, and the women of Soroptimist International for recognizing the merits of this storytelling project. The late Aparna Sharma nurtured and believed in this project from its earliest stages to its near completion. That is just one of the many reasons she is so dearly missed.

Over the course of writing this book, another group of friends was continually there with a laugh, a listening ear, a glass of chardonnay, or tickets to a really good show at the Hideout. Thank you Patricia Fernandez, Marty Harper, Shifra Harris, Paul Hirsch and Alison Balis, Brian and Jan Hieggelke, Helen Kaplow, Jennifer and Mike Mitchell, Nobuko Nagaoka, Mike Siska, Tiphante Spencer and Jeremy Babinet, Lee Tracey and Joel Fromer, Jared Weinstein, Tony Wittrock, and my "girl," Randi Shafton. To Matthew Jones, one of the most important constants in my life, thank you for the great gift that is your loyalty; and to Jill DiCicco, thank you for showing me, through your lifelong example, how to respond to someone who is suffering.

A special thanks to my father, David S. Ream, who taught me early on that "iconoclast" can be the most beautiful word in the English language; to my mother, Melva Luker, and stepfather, Joe Luker, who believed in this book enough to turn their home into a writer's retreat for two summers running; and to my brother and sister, Robert K. Ream and Kary Ream, who are always my most important touchstones. And to Jules, Arline, and Cami: Know that this book is an expression of my hope that the world you grow old in will be a kinder and more just place.

Finally, this book would not exist without two people who each play an outsize role in my life and my work. Patricia Evans's gorgeous photographic images say as much about her as they do about the women and men she photographs. Her compassion is her defining quality—her photographic subjects feel it, and her friends and colleagues feel it even more—and that compassion has made partnering with her a privilege and a joy (she gets extra points for always being willing to read the map).

In the wake of my own experience with violence, no person played a larger role in helping me rebuild my life than R. Clifton Spargo.

The idea for this book was sparked over a decade later—the result of hundreds of our usually late-night, listening-to-rock-music conversations. During these last, often lonely months of writing, Cliff's editorial suggestions, as he read every word of this manuscript, served as a reminder, though I didn't really need one, that his mind is as huge as his heart. I am grateful for all of the roles that he has played in my life.

Appendix: The Statistics Behind the Stories

Sexual Violence in the United States and Beyond Our Borders

Listening to survivors is the best way to learn about how rape and abuse affects those who have lived through it, but a large and credible body of research tells an equally serious story. What follows is a sourced, data-driven overview of the scope and scale of sexual violence nationally and globally. Please note that any review of statistics or "facts" about sexual violence should be done with this in mind: rape, incest, and all forms of sexual abuse remain vastly underreported crimes. Yet even with that caveat, the statistics that follow are both heartbreaking and humbling, reminding us of the important work we have to do to end sexual violence.

Sexual violence against women worldwide

Globally, 35 percent of women have experienced either non-partner sexual violence or intimate partner physical or sexual violence.[*]

Sexual violence against women in the United States

Nearly one in five women in the United States will be raped at some point in their lifetime.[†]

---

[*]World Health Organization, *Global and Regional Estimates of Violence Against Women: Prevalence and Health Effects of Intimate Partner Violence and Non-Partner Sexual Violence*, 2013, http://apps.who.int.

[†]M. Black et al., *The National Intimate Partner and Sexual Violence Survey (NISVS): 2010 Summary Report* (Atlanta: National Center for Injury Prevention and Control, Centers for Disease Control and Prevention, 2011).

Nearly half of all women (44.6 percent)—more than fifty-three million—experience sexual violence other than rape during their lives.*

Nine of ten victims of rape in the United States are female.†

The lifetime prevalence of rape varies by race and ethnicity:‡

- African American women: 22 percent
- Hispanic women: 15 percent
- Multiracial women: 33 percent
- Native American women: 27 percent
- White women: 19 percent

Sexual violence against men in the United States

One in seventy-one men will be raped at some point in their lives. This equals 1.6 million men in the United States.§

Over one in five men (22.2 percent)—more than twenty-five million—experience sexual violence other than rape in their lifetime.**

Sexual violence against children in the United States

Twenty-five percent of girls will be sexually abused before their eighteenth birthday.††

Nearly one in six boys will be sexually abused before they turn eighteen.

An estimated 325,000 children per year are at risk of becoming victims of commercial sex exploitation.‡‡

The average age of entry into prostitution is twelve to fourteen for girls and eleven to thirteen for boys.§§

---

*Black et al., *The National Intimate Partner and Sexual Violence Survey*.

†US Department of Justice, *2003 National Crime Victimization Survey*, 2003.

‡Black et al., *The National Intimate Partner and Sexual Violence Survey*.

§Ibid.

**Ibid.

††D. Finkelhor et al., "Sex Abuse in a National Survey of Adult Men and Women: Prevalence, Characteristics, and Risk Factors," *Child Abuse and Neglect* 14 (1990): 19-28.

‡‡National Coalition to Prevent Child Abuse and Exploitation, *National Plan to Prevent the Sexual Abuse and Exploitation of Children*, 2012, http://www.preventtogether.org/.

§§Ibid.

How often do victims report and how often are perpetrators convicted?

Only 5-20 percent of rapes are reported to police.[*]
A mere 5 percent of rapes result in a conviction.
Three percent of rapes result in incarceration of a perpetrator.

Who commits sexual violence?

Fourteen percent of rape victims were raped by a stranger.[†]
Fifty-one percent were raped by a man who was a current or former intimate partner.
Forty-one percent were raped by an acquaintance.

What are the effects of sexual violence?

Eighty-one percent of women and 35 percent of men who have been raped report either short- or long-term effects, such as posttraumatic stress disorder (PTSD).[‡]
The World Health Organization reported in 2002 that victims of rape are:

- three times more likely to suffer from depression
- thirteen times more likely to abuse alcohol
- twenty-six times more likely to abuse drugs
- four times more likely to contemplate suicide

Twenty-two percent of women who have been raped within the past twenty years live in poverty, compared to only 15 percent of those who have not been victims.[§]

What is intimate partner violence and how often does it occur?

Intimate partner violence includes sexual violence but also includes physical violence.

---

[*]Kimberly A. Lonsway and Joanne Archambault, "The 'Justice Gap' for Sexual Assault Cases: Future Directions for Research and Reform," *Violence Against Women* 18, no. 2 (2012): 145–68.

[†]Black et al., *The National Intimate Partner and Sexual Violence Survey.*
[‡]Ibid.

[§]Rebecca M. Loya, *Economic Consequences of Sexual Violence: Implications for Public Policy and Service Provision*, 2012. http://counterquo.org.

Thirty-six percent of women in the United States have experienced intimate partner violence at some point in their lives. That equals about forty-two million US women who have experienced some form of violence at the hands of an intimate partner.[*]

Thirty percent of women globally have experienced intimate partner violence in their lifetime.[†]

Both in the United States and globally, as many as 38 percent of murders of women have been committed by their intimate partners.[‡]

A word about words: Making sense of facts and statistics

Understanding statistics means understanding definitions. *Rape* and *sexual assault* have varying legal definitions, often changing by jurisdiction. Research studies can define *rape* and *sexual assault* in different ways. When using or comparing statistics, it is important to understand how the terms were defined when the research was conducted. The following definitions can serve as a general guide for you.

What is sexual assault? Sexual assault refers to any unwanted sexual contact. It can include penetration of a mouth, penis, or anus. It can also include kissing, fondling, grabbing, groping, and touching.

What is rape? In general, rape refers to completed penetration of a vagina, mouth or anus by a penis, finger, or object. Some studies—especially older ones—only include vaginal penetration and/or require an element of force for an act to be counted as rape. Such narrow definitions are now largely rejected by advocates and the legal community.

Sexual violence is the broadest term, encompassing rape, sexual assault, intimate partner violence, incest, child sexual abuse, and other forms of sexual violence.

[*]Black et al., *The National Intimate Partner and Sexual Violence Survey.*
[†]World Health Organization, *Global and Regional Estimates of Violence Against Women.*
[‡]Ibid.; Federal Bureau of Investigation, *Crime in the United States, 2010.*

RESOURCES

Get help. Get engaged. And get creative in the fight to end sexual violence.

Get help. Free, confidential, and 24/7 support is available for you right now. Please reach out if you or someone you know has been a victim of violence.

If you have been raped or sexually abused, call the National Sexual Assault Hotline at 1-800-656-HOPE, or visit the online hotline at rainn.org.

If you are a victim of domestic violence, call the National Domestic Violence Hotline at 1-800-799-7233.

If you are a victim of sex trafficking, call the National Human Trafficking Hotline at 1-888-373-7888 or text to BeFree (233733).

If you are seeking holistic support to heal, the Breathe Network connects survivors of sexual violence to trauma-informed, sliding-scale, holistic healing arts practitioners. thebreathenetwork.org

If you need legal help or advice, Victim Rights Law Center, the first national nonprofit law center solely dedicated to serving the needs of rape and sexual assault victims, can work with you to explore your options. victimrights.org

Get engaged. There are hundreds of inspiring organizations working to end sexual violence and trafficking. Consider this list merely a starting point.

Abused Deaf Women's Advocacy Services empowers female and male Deaf and Deaf-Blind survivors of domestic violence, sexual assault, and harassment to transform their lives while striving to change the beliefs and behaviors that foster and perpetuate violence. adwas.org

A Call to Men works to create a world where all men and boys are loving and respectful and all women and girls are safe from sexual violence, domestic violence, and trafficking. acalltomen.org

Amnesty International is a global movement of people fighting injustice and promoting human rights, including the right to live free of sexual violence. Their work on behalf of Native American rape victims and the Women of Atenco, Mexico, has been groundbreaking. amnestyusa.org

Break the Cycle provides comprehensive dating abuse prevention programs exclusively to young people, making safe and healthy relationships a right and a reality. breakthecycle.org

Coalition Against Trafficking in Women is a United Nations nongovernmental organization that engages in advocacy, education, and prevention programs for victims of trafficking and prostitution in the United States and across the globe. catwinternational.org

CounterQuo is a collective of anti-rape advocates from the worlds of advocacy, law, media, and public health seeking to challenge the status quo on sexual violence by fostering new and nontraditional alliances and information sharing. counterquo.org

End Violence Against Women International envisions a world where gender-based violence is unacceptable, where perpetrators are held accountable, and where victims receive the compassion, support, and justice they deserve. evawintl.org

Equality Now works for the protection and promotion of the human rights of women and girls worldwide, documenting violence and discrimination and mobilizing international action to support efforts to stop these abuses. equalitynow.org

Faith Trust Institute is a national, multifaith, multicultural training and education organization with global reach working to end sexual and domestic violence by engaging communities of faith in the fight. faithtrustinstitute.org

Futures Without Violence creates groundbreaking education programs, professional training programs, and public actions designed to end violence against women, children, and families around the world. futureswithoutviolence.org

Half the Sky Movement is cutting across platforms to ignite the change needed to put an end to the oppression of and violence against women and girls worldwide. halftheskymovement.org

Hollaback is a movement to end street harassment powered by a network of activists from across the globe. Its members ignite public conversations and develop innovative strategies to ensure equal access to public spaces. ihollaback.org

Human Rights Watch is one of the world's leading independent organizations dedicated to defending and protecting human rights. Their advocacy effort raising awareness of the rape kit backlog in the United States is especially of note. hrw.org

Joyful Heart Foundation seeks to heal, educate, and empower survivors of sexual assault, domestic violence, and child abuse, and to shed light onto the darkness that surrounds these issues. joyfulheartfoundation.org

Know Your IX is a survivor-driven campaign that aims to educate US college students about their rights under Title IX to have campus rape or sexual assault charges investigated and resolved. knowyourix.org

Legal Momentum advances and protects the rights of women and girls though education, litigation, and public policy. Started in 1970, it is the oldest organization of its kind in the United States. legalmomentum.org

Man Up Campaign seeks to engage youth in a global movement to end gender-based violence and advance gender equality, transforming communities, nations, and the world. manupcampaign.org

Men Can Stop Rape mobilizes men to use their strength for creating cultures free from violence, especially men's violence against women and girls. mencanstoprape.org

Move to End Violence seeks to improve the status and well-being of girls and women worldwide, who too often experience violence, poverty, and discrimination simply because they are born female. movetoendviolence.org

National Alliance to End Sexual Violence is the voice in Washington, DC, for state coalitions and local programs working to end sexual violence and support survivors. endsexualviolence.org

National Organization of Sisters of Color Ending Sexual Assault is developing action strategies that incorporate and address the multiple layers of discrimination that are faced by women and communities of color. sisterslead.org

Office on Violence Against Women at the US Department of Justice provides federal leadership in developing the nation's capacity to reduce violence against women and administer justice for and strengthen services to victims of gender-based violence. ovw.usdoj.gov

PAVE (Promoting Awareness, Victim Empowerment) is a national, grassroots nonprofit. PAVE uses education and action to shatter the silence of sexual and domestic violence including sexual abuse, rape, sexual assault and intimate partner violence. pavingtheway.net

Polaris Project is committed to combating human trafficking and modern-day slavery, and to strengthening the anti-trafficking movement through a comprehensive approach. polarisproject.org

RAINN (Rape, Abuse and Incest National Network) is the nation's largest anti–sexual assault organization, with programs to prevent sexual assault, help victims, and ensure that rapists are brought to justice. rainn.org

Service Women's Action Network (SWAN) is transforming US military culture by securing equal opportunity and freedom to serve without discrimination, harassment, or sexual assault. servicewomen.org

The Voices and Faces Project brings the names, faces, and stories of survivors of sexual violence and trafficking to the attention of the public through a series of creative, documentary, and public-outreach initiatives. voicesandfaces.org

We Will Speak Out is a community of faith-based NGOs (nongovernmental organizations) from across the globe who are committed to empowering women and girls, transforming relationships between women and men, and ensuring that the voices of survivors of sexual violence—women, girls, men, and boys—are central to their work. wewillspeakout.org

1in6 seeks to help men who have had unwanted or abusive sexual experiences in childhood live happier, healthier lives through a series of outreach and healing programs. 1in6.org

Get creative. Advocacy and direct service are critical to the fight to end sexual violence. So is creativity. Dare to do something different.

A Long Walk Home uses art therapy and the visual and performing arts to end violence against girls and women, while creating forums through which the public can learn about healing from and preventing gender violence. alongwalkhome.org

A Window Between Worlds is a US-based nonprofit dedicated to using art as a healing tool for survivors of domestic violence, sexual assault, and interpersonal trauma. awbw.org

Angel Band Project inspires people to engage with the issue of sexual violence through the transformative power of music, creating a society that's willing to listen and ready to change. angelbandproject.org

Art Works for Change creates international contemporary art exhibitions that address critical social justice and environmental issues. Its groundbreaking exhibition, *Off the Beaten Path: Violence, Women and Art*, has traveled the globe to engage the public in the fight to end gender-based violence. artworksforchange.org

Art Works Projects uses design and the arts to raise awareness of and educate the public about significant human rights and environmental issues, including rape and sex trafficking in global and local communities. artworksprojects.org

The Bandana Project is a groundbreaking arts initiative that uses the bandana as a symbol of solidarity to end workplace sexual violence and abuse against immigrant and farmworker women. E-mail: monica@cdmigrante.org

Breakthrough. Working out of centers in India and the United
  States, Breakthrough uses the power of arts, media, pop culture,
  and community mobilization to inspire people to build a world in
  which all people live up to their full potential. breakthrough.tv

Clothesline Project is a vehicle for women affected by sexual violence to give voice to their experiences and to share those stories
  in a way that changes minds and hearts. clotheslineproject.org

International Museum of Women is an online museum that inspires creativity, awareness and action on vital global issues for
  women and girls, including the fight to end gender-based violence. imow.org

One Billion Rising is a global call to women survivors of violence
  to break the silence and release their stories through art, dance,
  marches, ritual, song, spoken word, testimonies, and whatever
  feels right for them. onebillionrising.org

The OpEd Project seeks to increase the number of women thought
  leaders contributing to key commentary forums—which feed all
  other media, and drive thought leadership across all industries—
  to a tipping point. theopedproject.org

Project Unbreakable is a crowd-sourced photography project that
  seeks to increase awareness of the issues surrounding sexual assault and encourage the act of healing through art and photography. projectunbreakable.tumblr.com

The Stories We Tell is North America's first two-day testimonial
  writing workshop for survivors of sexual violence, domestic
  violence, and trafficking who seek to use their stories to create personal and political transformation. voicesandfaces.org/
  writingworkshop.html

Take Back the Night has become internationally known for almost three decades as a way to take a public stand against sexual

violence and speak out against what it means to victims, families, and communities. takebackthenight.org

Time to Tell is a child sexual abuse prevention project and storytelling initiative grounded in the core values of healing, social justice, and joy. It's time to tell your story. timetotell.org

V-Day is a global activist movement to end violence against women and girls through creative events that generate broader attention for the fight to stop rape, battery, incest, female genital mutilation (FGM), and sex slavery. vday.org

Women, Action and the Media (WAM!) is building a robust, effective, inclusive movement for gender justice in the media, one that represents the diversity of women's lives and stories. women actionmedia.org

Women's Media Center works to create a level playing field for women and girls in media through media monitoring, training, the creation of original content, and activism. womensmedia center.com